WALKS IN
THE COUNTRY
NEAR LONDON

CHRISTOPHER SOMERVILLE

NEW
HOLLAND

This book is dedicated with warm affection to Howard Richmond and Robin Rubenstein and their sons Matthew and Michael, hoping that they will venture out of London to enjoy these walks.

This edition published in 2012 by
New Holland Publishers (UK) Ltd
London • Cape Town • Sydney • Auckland
First published in 2003

www.newhollandpublishers.com

Garfield House
86–88 Edgware Road
London W2 2EA
United Kingdom

Wembley Square First Floor
Solan Road Gardens
Cape Town 8001
South Africa

Unit 1, 66 Gibbes Street
Chatswood, NSW 2067
Australia

218 Lake Road
Northcote
Auckland
New Zealand

ISBN 978 1 84773 946 9

Publisher: Guy Hobbs
Editor: Clare Hubbard
Layout and Design: Lucy Parissi
Cover Design: Stephanie Foti
Cartography: William Smuts
Production: Marion Storz
Printer: Toppan Leefung Printing Ltd (China)

Publishers' Note: While every care has been taken to ensure that the information in this book was as accurate as possible at the time of going to press, the publishers and author accept no responsibility for any loss, injury or inconvenience sustained by anyone using this book.

CONTENTS

KEY TO MAPS

Each of the walks in the book is accompanied by a map on which the route is shown in blue. Places of interest along the walk, such as historic buildings, churches and pubs, are clearly identified. Where necessary, specific route directions have also been included on the maps. In both the text and the maps, certain features and national trails have been abbreviated as follows:

FP	Footpath	SHT	Swale Heritage Trail
PB	Public Bridleway	NDW	North Downs Way
BW	Byway	GW	Greensand Way
PH	Public House	GWLR	Greensand Way Link Route
NT	National Trust	SVW	Stour Valley Walk
BT	John Bunyan Trail	MVW	Medway Valley Walk
IW	Icknield Way	EVW	Eden Valley Walk
CW	Chiltern Way	VW	Vanguard Way
EW	Essex Way	PW	Pilgrims' Way
RVW	Roach Valley Way	HW	Hangers Way
DVP	Darent Valley Path	WW	Wayfarer's Walk

Although every effort has been taken to ensure that these maps are clear and correct, Ordnance Survey grid references are provided at key parts of the route for each walk. Details of relevant Ordnance Survey maps are supplied at the start of each walk.

The following is a key to the symbols used on the maps.

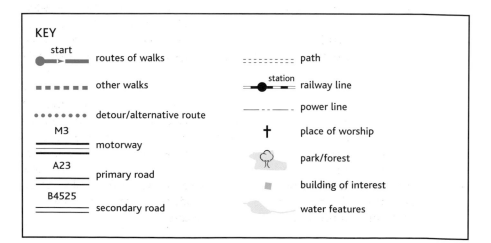

KEY

start — routes of walks

other walks

detour/alternative route

M3 — motorway

A23 — primary road

B4525 — secondary road

path

station — railway line

power line

place of worship

park/forest

building of interest

water features

INTRODUCTION

Since the first edition of *Walks in the Country Near London* came out in 2003, country walking has grown exponentially in popularity. More and more Londoners and others who live within the orbit of the capital are turning to this inexpensive, all-absorbing, invigorating activity.

In those few years since 2003 a lot of things have changed in the beautiful countryside around London. There has been a rash of house building and road construction. Cars have got bigger and faster. Off-road drivers have spoiled some green lanes for walkers. So I have re-walked the routes in this book, reshaping some and replacing others to maintain their status as top walks for Londoners and their country cousins. And here I want to give huge thanks and praise to my daughter Ruth Somerville, who has very kindly (and nobly, in the depths of a bitter winter) walked these routes independently to verify them, reporting back with incredible accuracy and efficiency.

Four of the original walks have been dropped because some of their sections along roads have become too dangerous to recommend – these are Bayford–Brickendon in Hertfordshire; Charing–Pluckley in Kent; Paddock Wood–Capel, also in Kent; and Wanborough–Compton in Surrey. I've chosen four new walks, each starting at a railway station, to replace them. Three of these have been adapted from walks previously published in my long-out-of-print book *Country Walks Near London* (Simon & Schuster 1994): a wander through Buckinghamshire's gorgeous Chess Valley (Walk 5, starting from the tube station at Chalfont and Latimer); an exploration of the Medway Estuary in north Kent around Lower Halstow (Walk 15, with three stunning churches); and a circuit through the wooded Kentish Weald (Walk 16) that takes in the moated medieval manor house of Ightham Mote. The new Surrey walk (Walk 22) is a beauty, too, around the farmlands and villages in the shadow of the North Downs near Reigate.

A few walks have been rerouted over short sections to avoid dangerous or unpleasant roads: Walks 6, 18 and 25. Dedicated followers of the walks from the previous edition will spot other tweaks. Obviously you should always exercise care when walking along roads and crossing roads and railway lines.

These country rambles are not designed for masochistic tread-till-you're-dead hikers. Almost all the walks are between 6 and 10 miles (10–16km) – a morning's worth if you are reasonably fit and don't want to stop en route, an easy day if you are going to take your time and explore a bit. A couple of longer walks have been included for those who are in need of a good stride out. Be warned, however, that outside of the summer months and in wet conditions, several of the walks can be very muddy and waterproof footwear is highly recommended.

You don't need to be a navigation expert: the comprehensive instructions have been carefully designed, not just to steer experienced country walkers from one village to the next, but to get complete beginners from one stile to the next. The Ordnance Survey of Great Britain produces far and away the best walkers' maps in the world, and you are strongly advised to take the relevant OS map to supplement the sketch maps provided in this book.

Advice on exactly which OS map you'll need is included in the information section at the head of each walk. The Explorer series covers the area at twice the scale of the Landranger series, and also includes field boundaries and other helpful detail. Ordnance Survey national grid reference numbers are included within the text at all points where you might need to check your position. If you want to slip a compass into your pocket, it might be reassuring – though not really necessary.

Distances should be treated as approximate – for example: 'In 100 yards (100m) turn left' does not mean a distance exactly measured at 100 yards rather than 99 or 101, but 100 rather than 50 or 150. By the same token, conversion from imperial to metric measurements and vice versa is also approximate. One hundred yards is actually 91 metres, but I hope you know what I mean by '100 yards (100m)'!

Other useful advice given in each information section includes the length of the walk, where you start and finish, how to get there from central London by rail (and by road, if you must), where you can get a drink and something to eat en route, and the various special features and attractions along the way. More detailed information, including addresses, telephone numbers, websites and opening hours, is given in Further Information (pages 192–200) for features open to the public, such as stately homes, castles, museums and pubs. It's a wise plan to phone before you set out to double-check on prices, opening and food-serving times, as these can and do change. Don't forget to carry your National Trust, English Heritage and other membership cards that give you free entry, as several of the attractions are run by these organisations. Many churches are kept locked; contact details are given for these, too, so that with a little forward planning you can get in.

I have personally walked every yard of these 25 rambles. However, since things in the countryside change all the time, it is possible that small details may have altered by the time you set out. If so, or if you find any other inaccuracies in this book, please let me know via the publishers. I will gladly acknowledge your help and incorporate your amendments in any future editions of *Walks in the Country Near London*. Have a wonderful time!

Christopher Somerville

Opposite: Footpath fingerposts, like this one on the Ridgeway National Trail, point the way for experienced hikers and complete beginners alike.

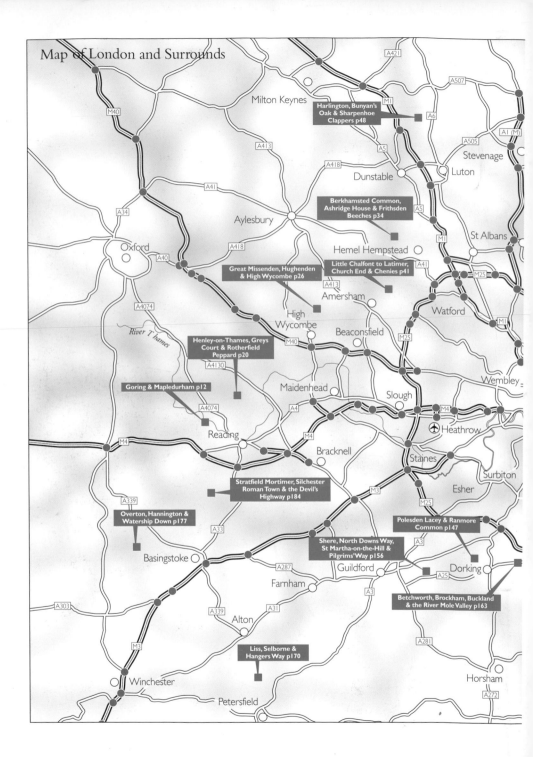

Map of London and Surrounds

Milton Keynes

Harlington, Bunyan's
Oak & Sharpenhoe
Clappers p48

Stevenage

Dunstable

Luton

Aylesbury

St Albans

Berkhamsted Common,
Ashridge House & Frithsden
Beeches p34

Oxford

Hemel Hempstead

Great Missenden, Hughenden
& High Wycombe p26

Little Chalfont to Latimer,
Church End & Chenies p41

Amersham

Watford

River Thames

High
Wycombe

Beaconsfield

Henley-on-Thames, Greys
Court & Rotherfield
Peppard p20

Wembley

Goring & Mapledurham p12

Maidenhead

Slough

Heathrow

Reading

Bracknell

Staines

Surbiton

Esher

Stratfield Mortimer, Silchester
Roman Town & the Devil's
Highway p184

Polesden Lacey & Ranmore
Common p147

Overton, Hannington &
Watership Down p177

Shere, North Downs Way,
St Martha-on-the-Hill &
Pilgrims' Way p156

Dorking

Basingstoke

Farnham

Guildford

Betchworth, Brockham, Buckland
& the River Mole Valley p163

Alton

Liss, Selborne &
Hangers Way p170

Horsham

Winchester

Petersfield

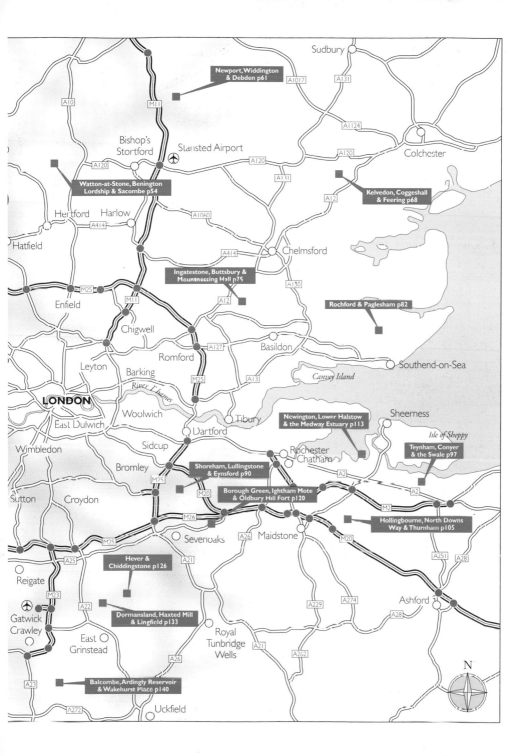

Newport, Widdington & Debden p61

Watton-at-Stone, Benington Lordship & Sacombe p54

Kelvedon, Coggeshall & Feering p68

Ingatestone, Buttsbury & Mountnessing Hall p75

Rochford & Paglesham p82

Newington, Lower Halstow & the Medway Estuary p113

Teynham, Conyer & the Swale p97

Shoreham, Lullingstone & Eynsford p90

Borough Green, Ightham Mote & Oldbury Hill Fort p120

Hollingbourne, North Downs Way & Thurnham p105

Hever & Chiddingstone p126

Dormansland, Haxted Mill & Lingfield p133

Balcombe, Ardingly Reservoir & Wakehurst Place p140

11

1. GORING & MAPLEDURHAM

Enjoy the beech and oak woods, the lush green grazing meadows and the glorious river scenery along a most delectable stretch of the Thames Valley. Take a break in the beautifully preserved old village of Mapledurham, and visit the lovely and atmospheric Elizabethan country house where Roman Catholic priests were hidden in times of persecution. Kenneth Grahame used Mapledurham as inspiration for Toad Hall in *The Wind In The Willows* (1908), and the book's illustrator Ernest Shepard based several of his pictures on the old mill and weir. This twist of countryside where the Thames snakes through the narrow confines of the Goring Gap and on towards Reading was one of Grahame's favourite parts of the river. He lies buried in Pangbourne.

START:	Goring and Streatley Station
FINISH:	Pangbourne Station
LENGTH OF WALK:	12 miles (19km)
OS MAPS:	1:50,000 Landranger 175; 1:25,000 Explorer 170, 159
TRAVEL:	By rail from London Paddington, change at Reading (49 mins); by road – M25 (Jct 15), M4 (Jct 12), A4 through Theale for 1 mile (1.6km), A340 to Pangbourne, A329 to Goring.
FEATURES:	Thames Path National Trail; Goring Gap; views along the Thames; Isambard Kingdom Brunel's railway bridge at Gatehampton; Bottom Wood and Farm; Mapledurham House and Mill and village; Whitchurch Toll Bridge; Pangbourne.
REFRESHMENTS:	Mapledurham House tea room; pubs and cafés in Goring and Whitchurch; The Swan, Pangbourne.

Opposite: The watermill at Mapledurham, which dates back to medieval times, is said to have inspired Ernest Shepard's illustrations to Kenneth Grahame's famous children's book The Wind in the Willows.

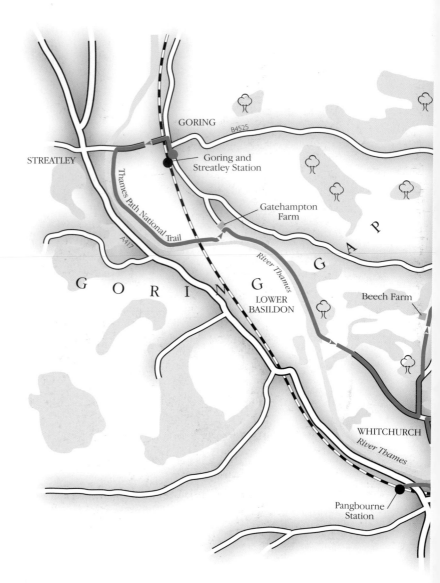

GORING

STREATLEY

B4525

Goring and
Streatley Station

Thames Path National Trail

A417

Gatehampton
Farm

River Thames

G O R I N   G   G   A   P

LOWER
BASILDON

Beech Farm

WHITCHURCH

River Thames

Pangbourne
Station

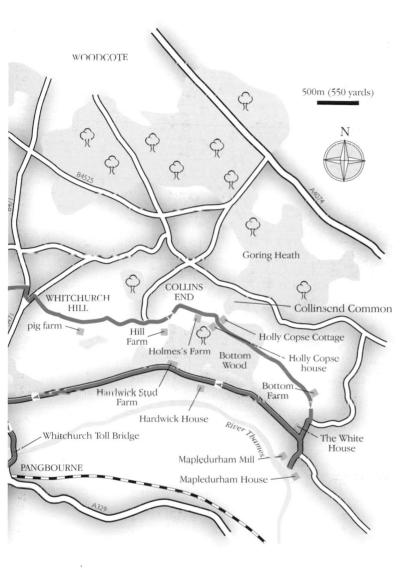

500m (550 yards)

N

WOODCOTE

B4525

A4074

Goring Heath

COLLINS
END

Collinsend Common

WHITCHURCH
HILL

pig farm

Hill
Farm

Holly Copse Cottage

Holmes's Farm

Bottom
Wood

Holly Copse
house

Hardwick Stud
Farm

Bottom
Farm

Hardwick House

River Thames

The White
House

Whitchurch Toll Bridge

PANGBOURNE

Mapledurham Mill

Mapledurham House

A329

15

Cross over the platform bridge at Goring and Streatley Station (603806), walk left up the approach road following the Thames Path sign, and keep ahead, to bear left in 200 yards (200m) across the railway bridge and on down to the bridge over the River Thames (596808). This river crossing between Goring and Streatley is an ancient one. The prehistoric Ridgeway or Icknield Way fords the Thames here, and a ferry of sorts was operating from the time of King Henry I in the early 12th century. There are some fine old Georgian houses across the river in Streatley.

Thames Path National Trail

Just before the bridge, opposite the post office, a slip road leads to the left (fingerpost 'Whitchurch 3.5 miles'), down beside the bridge and on to the Thames Path National Trail. From this point for the next 3½ miles (5.5km) to Whitchurch, navigation is easy – just follow the Thames Path waymarks. The Thames Path in its entirety shadows the course of the river for 180 miles (290km), from its humble source in a Gloucestershire meadow to the beginning of its great estuary at the Thames Flood Barrier in east London. The National Trail was officially opened in 1996, after almost a century's attempts to establish some kind of acknowledged route for walkers along the old towpath.

The Goring Gap

The path runs south from Goring along the east bank of the Thames, passing large Edwardian houses with beautifully kept lawns. You enter open countryside of broad grazing meadows, and soon pass under an impressive Victorian railway bridge in warm red brick blotched with lichens and stained by the weather (606796). It carries Isambard Kingdom Brunel's Great Western Railway line across the Thames, to squeeze with the river through the Goring Gap. This cleft in the chalk hills was forced through by rushing meltwater after the end of the last Ice Age. Once the breakthrough had occurred the meltwaters cut a narrow gorge in the chalk that gradually broadened out, perhaps 6,000 years ago. The Gap has the effect of pulling the downs dramatically close all of a sudden – the Berkshire Downs to the right across the river, and the Oxfordshire outliers of the Chiltern Hills at your left hand.

The path skirts the old ferry cottage at Gatehampton and continues in chalk woodland for a really beautiful mile (1.6km), with glimpses through the trees to the river below, before swinging inland (621786) through the southern shank of Hartslock Wood. Once out of the trees the path forks; bear left, following the Thames Path for a mile (1.6km) across the downs, at first as a track and then a tarmacked drive, before reaching the B471 (633775), ½ mile (0.75km) north of Whitchurch Toll Bridge (Thames Path fingerpost on opposite side of the road). Cross over on to the verge opposite to avoid the traffic and turn left up the road (please take care!) for some 400 yards (400m). At the war memorial cross back to the left side of the road and keep ahead up a slope. As the road below bends right, take the path through a gate away from the road and follow it along a field edge with woodland to your right (633780) for 400 yards (400m). Keep ahead to pass Beech Farm (634787). Cross the drive and the paddock beyond, then keep ahead through the kissing gate (Chiltern Way waymark) into woodland. Soon the path forks; bear left, following CW signs to the farm drive. Turn left up the drive and keep ahead to turn right along the B471 (637789).

In 150 yards (150m), opposite a thatched cottage, bear left; in 50 yards (50m) turn left again at a T-junction; in another 50 yards (50m) head right (FP sign on left side of the road) down a gravelly track. Pass a terrace of cottages, go through a kissing gate and follow the path across a field to the far left corner, where you bear right along a track (641786). In 250 yards (250m), keep ahead (three yellow arrow waymarks), following the CW. The next field ends at a lane (647785); bear right here to meet a road (649784). Turn left. In 300 yards (300m), at a sharp left bend (652785), bear right (CW). In 100 yards (100m), where the road swings right, keep ahead ('Collins End ½' FP/CW sign) through trees, dropping steeply down into a valley only to climb steeply up the other side, aiming for a house on the skyline.

Collinsend Common

At the top of the rise, 50 yards (50m) before the house, turn right across a stile, then left through a gate (CW) to a lane (657787) where you turn right. At Holmes's Farm, a 'Bridleway, Mapledurham 2' sign directs you forward, with a fence on your right, to a gate into a tarmac lane where Briar Cottage stands slightly to your right (661785) on the edge of Goring Heath. The whole area of Goring Heath was enclosed in 1812, depriving the commoners of their right to graze animals on common land. The thin scatter of houses across Collinsend Common, just beyond Holly Copse, shows how building went on all over the open land.

Follow the track right past Briar Cottage to Holly Copse house and Holly Copse Cottage beyond. Bear right on the track between the two houses (blue PB arrow), on to a gravel bridleway (soon turning chalky) that descends through the woods. At first this bridleway is very boggy, but it soon improves. Follow the PB signs. In the wood bottom (663783), where the track forks, do NOT take the path to the right up the slope, but keep ahead along the valley to leave the wood at a gate (666781).

Red Kites

Red kites have been reintroduced to the valley with great success, and one of the major highlights of the walk is to see these huge birds of prey circling around the valley slopes and perching on posts and trees.

Keep ahead south-east along the valley. In ¹/₂ mile (0.75km) pass Bottom Farm (672776) and continue south along the drive to a road (672773); keep ahead here to pass The White House (671770; fingerpost 'Whitchurch 2¹/₂ miles') and walk through Mapledurham village to Mapledurham House (670766).

Mapledurham House and Mill

A timber-framed 14th-century manor house stands on the site, but it is overshadowed by the great Tudor house built of red brick in 1580 by Michael Blount, courtier and Lieutenant of the Tower. Blount was a devout Roman Catholic, and must have been held in enormously high favour by Queen Elizabeth I to have been allowed to build himself such a sumptuous house at a time in English history when men of his religion were held to be no better than traitors. He was no trimmer, though. Many a brave priest infiltrating England from the Continent, at risk of a horrible death upon capture, came warily upriver to Mapledurham. One of the house's high gables overlooking the Thames is still studded with the oyster shells that were fixed there as a sign of a recusant or staunchly Catholic house. Mapledurham stands only 50 yards (50m) from the river, and could offer safe hiding for fugitives among its secret rooms and craftily hidden compartments. These included a noxious hole next to the privy – hard to bear for a man cooped up there for days on end, but guaranteed to put the sniffer dogs off.

On a tour of the house, along with elaborate 17th-century plasterwork and portraits of the dark-faced Blounts, you can see some of the many hidey-holes and a secret chapel under the eaves which would, if discovered, have got Michael Blount into very serious – probably terminal – trouble. There is also a much more luxurious chapel built in the 1790s in fashionable Strawberry Hill Gothic style. Horrific accounts of the bloodbaths accompanying the French Revolution had helped make the English more sympathetic to Catholic refugees, and no one raised objections when the Blounts invested in a new chapel to accommodate the many French émigrés who were making their way to Mapledurham in expectation of help and support.

The medieval watermill opposite the house was picturesque enough to inspire Ernest Shepard when he was looking for ideas for his marvellous illustrations to Kenneth Grahame's 1908 children's classic *The Wind In The Willows*. Some say that Grahame based Toad Hall upon Mapledurham. These days the restored mill grinds flour with the help of its oaken waterwheel. Outside the gates of Mapledurham lies the tiny one-street village, a calendar-photographer's dream of mellow red-brick cottages and almshouses.

Hardwick House and Stud Farm

From Mapledurham return to The

White House, to follow the PB sign ('Whitchurch 2½ miles') that points left along a track through the fields. In ½ mile (0.75km) you pass through the elaborately curlicued iron gates of Hardwick House (665776), and continue along the drive past the house itself, with glimpses over its hedge of mellow brick chimneys and gables. Pass the striking C-shaped, half-timbered stable block of Hardwick Stud Farm (654779) – if a friendly stable hand is around, you might even be allowed to stroke one of the horses, and you'll certainly see them grazing in the nearby meadows.

Pass through gates and keep ahead along a lane ('Whitchurch' sign).

Broad roadside verges, a raised track and sparse traffic make the next mile of road walking easy and pleasant. When you reach the B471 (634775) turn left through Whitchurch for ½ mile (0.75km), passing the Greyhound and Ferryboat pubs to cross the Thames by Whitchurch Toll Bridge (636768), one of only two still operating on the river. It's a free passage for walkers.

On the south bank bear right in 150 yards (150m) along a brick-walled alley. Keep along this narrow fenced and hedged path beside the Thames to reach the A329 opposite the entrance to Pangbourne Station (632767).

2. HENLEY-ON-THAMES, GREYS COURT & ROTHERFIELD PEPPARD

A gorgeous secluded valley – a favourite haunt of red kites – sinuates west from the famous rowing town of Henley-on-Thames, taking you to two of east Oxfordshire's most attractive small villages, Rotherfield Greys and Rotherfield Peppard. There is a chance to look over Greys Court – a historic house infused with bizarre stories. The return walk to Henley lies along ancient green lanes and trackways frequented by songbirds.

START AND FINISH: Henley-on-Thames Station

LENGTH OF WALK: 8½ miles (13.5km)

OS MAPS: 1:50,000 Landranger 175; 1:25,000 Explorer 171

TRAVEL: By rail from London Paddington (55 mins); by road – M4 (Jct 10), A321; or M40 (Jct 4), A404, A4155.

FEATURES: Henley-on-Thames waterfront; Knollys monuments in St Nicholas' Church, Rotherfield Greys; Greys Court (NT); Rotherfield Peppard Common; Pack and Prime Lane and Dog Lane.

REFRESHMENTS: Maltsters Arms PH, Rotherfield Greys; La Ruchetta restaurant, Red Lion PH, Rotherfield Peppard.

Henley-on-Thames has one of the most attractive waterfronts along the River Thames. During the Henley Royal Regatta, the crux of Henley's summertime social calendar, the waterfront is at its most colourful and animated, but it's worth the two-minute detour from the railway station at any time of year.

From Henley-on-Thames Station (764823) walk to the Imperial Hotel. Turn right if you want to view the waterfront from Henley Bridge; otherwise turn left to cross a road and keep forward (762823 – 'Holy Trinity Church' fingerpost) up a tarmac path. Bear right by gates at the top along a

Opposite: Greys Court, so rich in romance and tragedy, also boasts beautiful walled gardens, which are open to the public throughout the summer months.

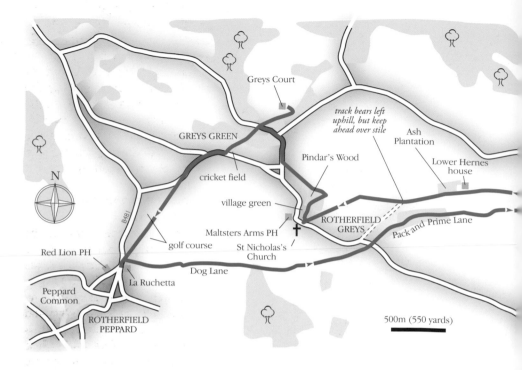

Greys Court

track bears left
uphill, but keep
ahead over stile

Ash
Plantation

GREYS GREEN

Pindar's Wood

Lower Hernes
house

cricket field

N

village green

ROTHERFIELD
GREYS

Pack and Prime Lane

Maltsters Arms PH

St Nicholas's
Church

golf course

Red Lion PH

Dog Lane

La Ruchetta

Peppard
Common

ROTHERFIELD
PEPPARD

500m (550 yards)

walled lane to a road junction (759824). Cross over and head down Deanfield Avenue, turning immediately left along a shady path (FP fingerpost). In 350 yards (350m) join a road and keep forward, to turn right along Tilebarn Close. At the top (753822) bear left into the fields along a track between a fence and a hedge (follow 'Rotherfield Greys' sign). In ⅓ mile (0.5km) cross Pack and Prime Lane by a stile (748825) and keep forward on a fenced track that curves west along the valley floor.

Red Kites

As soon as you leave Henley behind, the ground steepens to green grassy shoulders under fine beeches and oaks.

The valley leading west curves with the soft chalk; it has a broad shallow floor between sloping sides that rise smoothly to ridges parallel to the path. There are plantations of larch, ash, beech and fir trees, and huge specimen beech and cedar in the valley.

This is an excellent place to spot red kites. Since the reintroduction of these dramatically beautiful birds of prey to the Chiltern Hills at the end of the 20th century – an act of conservation that redressed centuries of persecution by gamekeepers, farmers and egg-collectors – numbers have soared. Over 300 pairs were reported to be thriving in the Chilterns by the year 2000. Red kites have a russet-red back, black-lined

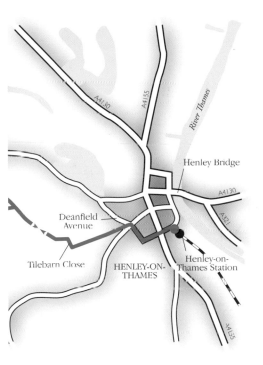

Henley Bridge

A4130

A4155

A4130

River Thames

Deanfield Avenue

A321

Tilebarn Close

HENLEY-ON-THAMES

Henley-on-Thames Station

A4155

Continue with the hedge on your left through the following gate, and in 100 yards (100m) turn left over a stile (732826 – yellow arrow) through the hedge. Turn right and keep ahead for 100 yards (100m), then bear left up the slope with a fence on your left. At the crest of the hill, pass the corner of Pindar's Wood (728824) and continue across Rotherfield Greys village green to the road and church (726823).

Rotherfield Greys and the Naughty Knollyses

There are fine beech trees around the village green, and a beacon complete with its fire basket. The Maltster's Arms is a pleasant pub. In the flint-built Norman church stands the imposing Knollys tomb. Sir Francis Knollys and his wife in splendid Elizabethan dress lie between marble pillars, while their son Sir William Knollys and his spouse kneel on the roof. A row of piously kneeling daughters is lined up along the tomb edge; their brothers are hidden from view on the far side of the monument.

The Knollyses owned Greys Court (see below), and were a colourful bunch. Sir Francis was one of Queen Elizabeth I's right-hand men; his wife was the sovereign's cousin. Their son Sir William seems to have been quite a nasty piece of work. Some say that William Shakespeare based the devious character of Malvolio on Sir William Knollys. But Knollys had his troubles too – it was said that his wife had so many affairs that all her children were declared illegitimate. This seems

wings and a deeply forked tail that tilts to every movement of the air. When they hover, the ends of the wings open into 'fingers' like those of a golden eagle. They seem remarkably unconcerned by the proximity of walkers, and will hover so closely overhead that you can hear their wings flap like yacht sails in a breeze.

Pass through the skirt of Ash Plantation below Lower Hernes house, keeping ahead and ignoring side turns (Hernes Estate sign). In 250 yards (250m), where the track snakes a little to the left (735825) and goes uphill to the left of a belt of trees in the valley bottom, leave the track and cross a stile beside the first of the trees (yellow arrow).

improbable, if the effigy on the tomb top bears anything like a fair resemblance to the lady.

It was Sir William's sister-in-law, Frances Howard, who really put the cat among the scandal pigeons. Beautiful and wilful, she divorced her husband the Earl of Essex and took up with Robert Carr, Earl of Somerset. When Sir Thomas Overbury, a courtier-poet and close acquaintance of Somerset's, tried to advise his friend against the liaison, the furious Frances pulled strings to have him clapped into the Tower of London, where he mysteriously died in 1613. Within a few months Frances had married Somerset, and for a time all seemed fine. But rumours began to fly. Two years later, arrested and accused of murdering Overbury, Frances admitted to having had the poet's food laced with poison.

The Somersets were spared sentence of death, but imprisoned in the Tower until 1621. Then a royal order released them, on condition that they live at Greys Court and refrain from travelling more than 3 miles from the house. For such a high-profile couple-at-court, this was disgrace of the deepest dye.

From the church, return diagonally across the village green, aiming for a stile on the edge of Pindar's Wood. Cross it, and descend through the wood. Cross the stile at the bottom (729826) and turn left along the wood edge. Continue over stiles and up a slope towards a road (725828). Turn right on a path that runs just below the road for 250 yards (250m), then cross the road to turn left along a side road. In 200 yards (200m) turn right (723832) up a drive to reach Greys Court (725834).

Greys Court

This very handsome late-Elizabethan manor house, where many of the Knollys/Howard shenanigans took place, stands in the courtyard of a 14th-century castle. The Great Tower, still a dominant feature, was built and crenellated by John, 1st Lord de Grey, around 1348. In the following century the castle passed to the Lovells, a family haunted by a curious fate. A Lovell bride, playing hide-and-seek at her wedding feast, became trapped in a trunk and was discovered years later, a skeleton still clothed in her wedding dress. Bizarrely, the last of the family, Francis, Viscount Lovell, is said to have met much the same end. Having rebelled against King Henry VIII, the fugitive hid from the king's search parties in the cellar after entrusting the key to a loyal servant. But this man was unluckily killed – and, as he had told no one where his master was, the wretched Lovell starved to death behind the locked cellar door.

The interior of Greys Court is a fascinating assemblage of different architectural periods, from the massive medieval style of the kitchens through Jacobean furnishings to superb 18th-century rococo plasterwork. Outside you'll find a wheelhouse with a preserved wheel for raising water from the 200-ft (61-m) well by donkey power, a Tudor building known as Bachelor's Hall ('*Melius nil coelibe vita*, nothing is sweeter than the celibate life' says the inscription over the door – a slogan with plenty of relevance, given the various marital dramas played out in these surroundings), and fine gardens with some rare trees.

Return down the drive to the road. Turn right for 20 yards (20m), then go left across a stile (Chiltern Way/CW marker) and over the field. Climb to cross a stile into a wood, and keep ahead up through the trees to cross another stile. Aim ahead to leave the wood (721831), and follow a path to cross Greys Green cricket field and turn right along the grass verge of a road. Pass a side turning on your right (718830), walk on for 100 yards (100m), then bear left through a gate ('CW Extension'). Turn right along the permissive bridleway, following the route of the road for 300 yards (300m); then keep ahead on the bridleway as it crosses a rough stretch of land and a tree plantation through the middle of a golf course (beware of flying golf balls!) for ½ mile (0.75km) to reach the B481 at La Ruchetta Italian restaurant in Rotherfield Peppard (710820).

Rotherfield Peppard Common

'Rotherfield' means 'the clearing of the hryther', 'hryther' being a Saxon word for cattle. Stone Age and Bronze Age tribes from the Thames Valley ventured into these uplands to collect the flints they lacked in their gravelly lowlands, but it was the people of the Dark Ages who made major inroads into the Chiltern wildwood for grazing purposes. Peppard Common,

just across the B481, is 56 acres (23ha) of carefully preserved common land, a remnant of open grazing that was cleared of trees centuries ago by axe and fire.

Dog Lane and Pack and Prime Lane

Long stretches of green lane – under the names of Dog Lane, followed by Pack and Prime Lane – lead from Rotherfield Peppard back towards Henley. Dog Lane is more like 'Bog Lane' in parts, running stickily between high hedges of blackthorn, hazel and field maple. In Pack and Prime Lane you may see and hear warblers, long-tailed tits, goldcrests and woodpeckers among the surrounding holly bushes and oak, ash and horse chestnut trees. This is a centuries-old trade and droving route that is delightful to idle along.

From Rotherfield Peppard follow Dog Lane up the left side of La Ruchetta ('Right Of Way' fingerpost, 'Restricted Byway'), and on for ¾ mile (1.25km). At a tarmac lane (723819) keep ahead for ⅓ mile (0.5km) to pass two houses on your right. Immediately after, turn right over a stile (728820 – double fingerpost); follow the left-hand of the two paths indicated, to cross the left-hand of two stiles in a fence. Aim well to the right of a house ahead, following the path to cross a stile and go over a road (733821 – FP fingerpost). Follow the bridleway along Pack and Prime Lane for a mile (1.6km) to the stile at 748825; turn right here, and retrace your steps to Henley Station.

3. GREAT MISSENDEN, HUGHENDEN & HIGH WYCOMBE

This beautiful walk, through Chiltern beech-woods and over Buckinghamshire farmland and downland slopes, runs south from the valley of the River Misbourne at Great Missenden. There are long stretches (sometimes very muddy) through mixed woodland as you drop down into the well-manicured and charming Hughenden Valley. The shadow of Benjamin Disraeli, twice prime minister at the height of the Victorian era, lies long hereabouts. Hughenden Manor was his home, and the statesman himself is buried by the wall of St Michael and All Angels Church in Hughenden. The walk ends with a long descent down a 'secret' lane into the heart of High Wycombe.

START:	Great Missenden Station
FINISH:	High Wycombe Station
LENGTH OF WALK:	9 miles (14km)
OS MAPS:	1:50,000 Landranger 175; 1:25,000 Explorers 181, 172
TRAVEL:	By rail from London Marylebone (40 mins); by road – M40 (Jct 1), A413.
FEATURES:	Lovely woods and lanes; beautiful Hughenden Valley; Disraeli and other memorials in St Michael and All Angels Church, Hughenden; Hughenden Manor (NT).
REFRESHMENTS:	Polecat Inn on the A4128 south of Prestwood (876994); Origins at the White Lion, Cryers Hill; restaurant and tea room at Hughenden Manor.

Mischievous Monks of Missenden

Great Missenden is a typically neat and well-looked-after Chiltern commuter village these days, but in pre-Reformation days, the Augustinian monks of Missenden Abbey seem to have enjoyed some high old times. Scandal and the monks were bedfellows on more than one occasion. In 1297, one of the novices cut his own throat rather than face the rigours of monastic life at Missenden; but discipline must have slackened over the next half-century, for during King Edward III's reign one of the monastery's abbots was hanged for clipping coins (the criminal practice of clipping small segments out of the rim of silver or gold coins, and making new coins out of the stolen shavings). By the time of the Reformation, the Missenden monks had become all but indistinguishable from ordinary villagers. One of them was spotted, according to a local report, lurching 'at midnight out of a house in the village in doublet and jerkin, with a sword by his side'. However, the Missenden monks were useful to the local community as physicians, prescribing such cures as marrowbone of horses and oil of black snails.

From the station platform (893013) climb the steps to the road and hairpin immediately back to your left down Trafford Road. Walk to the bottom of Trafford Road and turn right up a tarmac road.

View Over Great Missenden

At the top of the hill, pause to admire the view back over the church tower and the roofs of Great Missenden peeping out of the trees in the Misbourne Valley, with the slope of the valley rising beyond to a wooded ridge.

The lane levels out at the top of the hill. Bear left to pass View Farm (889007), and keep ahead along a tree-shaded bridleway for 350 yards (350m) (ignore a footpath on your right) to where the path swings left. Here, go through the gate (886005 – yellow blob waymark) and follow the path along the lower edge of Atkins Wood. In 350 yards (350m) leave the wood (yellow arrow on post) and cross a field diagonally left to a road (880001). Bear right for 10 yards (10m), then left down Church Path (PB fingerpost). Where the houses end, the bridleway keeps ahead but bear off the bridleway here to follow the footpath (879000 – FP fingerpost). After 10 yards (10m) the path forks; take the right-hand route southwards through Peterley Wood, following Chiltern Society white arrows painted on trees. Note that initially these are paired with footpath waymarks, but after a couple of hundred yards/metres they diverge and are tricky to spot – so keep your eyes peeled!

Peterley Wood

Peterley Wood was an uncultivated wasteland until the monks of Missenden Abbey hedged and ditched it in the late 12th century. Old beeches and tangles of holly grow on the level ground of what must have been common grazing, and you can still make out the shapes of the monks' earth banks and ditches.

At the far edge of the wood you meet a bridleway (878996) at a post with a blue 'BW' arrow pointing right and left in clear view of the wood edge. Turn left here, and keep following the white arrows. In 100 yards (100m) they diverge right from the bridleway again (find the arrow by looking for the pair of trees on your right-hand side). After 50 yards (50m) there are 'FP' and 'BW' waymarks on a tree (on your right-hand side, a bit away from the path). Walk to this tree and follow the path right out of the woods through a gate, then straight on up a fenced path to cross the A4128 at the Polecat Inn (876994). Walk down the right side of the pub (FP fingerpost); continue along a field edge and over a stile, then on across the next field down to a stile (872992) where you turn left along the road. In 150 yards (150m) turn right (FP fingerpost) on a path for 1 mile (1.6km) through Longfield Wood.

Longfield Wood

Longfield Wood, by contrast, is long and thin – a slender strip of mixed woodland a mile (1.6km) long but only a 100 yards (100m) wide for most of its length – and curves along the crest and sides of the steep valley whose contours it clings to like a second skin.

Follow the obvious path through the wood; in 500 yards (500m) it goes under power lines (869988), and in another 250 yards (250m) it reaches the edge of the wood. Here it dips to the right, downhill through bushes (yellow arrow). In another 400 yards (400m) you join a broad track (866983); keep forward near the upper edge of the wood. In another ¼ mile (0.4km), pass gateposts and keep ahead along a driveway to meet a road (870980).

Longfield Wood to St Michael and All Angels Church, Hughenden

Turn sharply back to your right along the road. In ¼ mile (0.5km), ignoring the first kissing gate to the left, turn left over a stile (866980 – FP fingerpost) and climb the hillside. Cross a stile at the top and keep forward to the corner of a wood (866976 – stile and Buckinghamshire County Council yellow arrow), where you turn left along the wooded grounds of Pipers Corner School. Cross a stile (yellow arrow) and continue across a field. In 150 yards (150m) turn right over a stile and cross the school drive (870976). Go down a fenced path and over a stile to cross another drive and go through an iron kissing gate (FP fingerpost). Continue over a field to cross a stile and bear right (872974) through the east end of Gomms Wood. In 80 yards (80m)

Opposite: Benjamin Disraeli bought 18th-century Hughenden Manor in 1847. He and his wife, Mary Anne, Viscountess Beaconsfield, adored the house and its gardens, woods and fields – a retreat from the hurly-burly of political London.

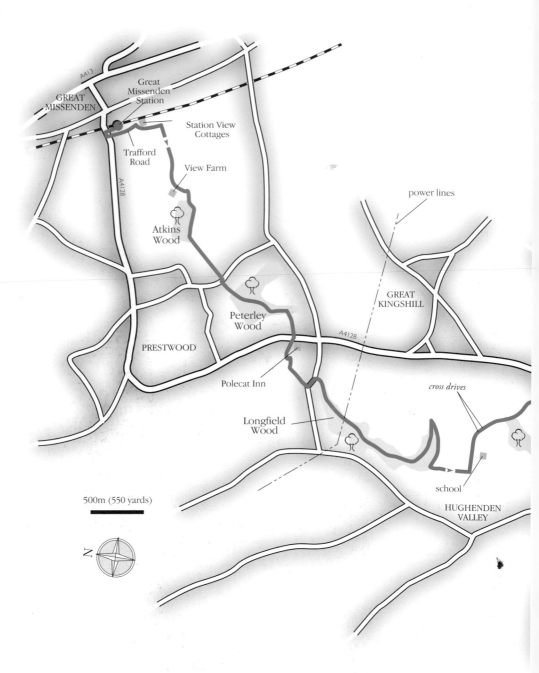

GREAT MISSENDEN

A413

Great Missenden Station

Station View Cottages

Trafford Road

View Farm

Atkins Wood

A4128

power lines

Peterley Wood

GREAT KINGSHILL

PRESTWOOD

A4128

Polecat Inn

cross drives

Longfield Wood

school

HUGHENDEN VALLEY

500m (550 yards)

N

WIDMER
END

CRYERS
HILL

Origins at the
White Lion PH

*turn sharp right
onto a green lane*

'secret'
lane

**HIGH
WYCOMBE**

barn

High Wycombe
Station

Gomms
Wood

Green
Hill Road

The
Greenway

Church of
St Michael
and All
Angels

Hughenden
Manor

small lake

A4128

A404

A40

turn up a slope, turn left, then keep ahead with a hedge on your left. At the far end of this field join a fenced path to reach the A4128 at Cryers Hill (875969). Just to your left are a post office/shop and Origins at the White Lion.

Turn right along the A4128 for 100 yards (100m), then cross the road and follow a path through the trees (FP fingerpost). Kissing gates and yellow arrows bring you along field edges and then through trees. In ⅓ mile (0.4km), ignore a confusing yellow arrow waymark on a gate on your right, and keep ahead along the top edge of a wood and then a green lane. At a stile (869960) turn right, then left along a field edge with a hedge on your right. Pass a barn (868958), and at the next hedge turn right (stile and blue arrow) to the A4128 (867955). Cross the road (with great care!) and turn left for 50 yards (50m), then right up the drive to St Michael and All Angels Church (864955).

The Disraelis and Hughenden

The Hughenden Valley is a rural Home Counties idyll, so neat and beautiful are its grassy meadows and well-kept woodlands, especially the 560 acres (227ha) of the Hughenden Estate owned and cared for by the National Trust. Benjamin Disraeli – leader of the Tory party, twice prime minister of Great Britain, successful novelist and incorrigible romantic – bought the estate in 1847 and grew to love it passionately during the 25 years he spent here with his wife Mary Anne, Viscountess Beaconsfield. The Disraelis were hands-on owners; they landscaped and planted the gardens and many of the woodlands, built a splendid set of stables (these now house the National Trust's ticket office, shop and tea rooms), and from 1862 remodelled the plain Georgian house of Hughenden Manor in dashing Gothic style. Disraeli made sure that a pinch of drama attended life at Hughenden – he armed the servants with revolvers to counter burglarious attempts, installed a flock of peacocks to amuse Mary Anne and appointed a little lad to the post of 'peacock-ward'.

A tour of Hughenden Manor brings the Disraelis to life with many personal touches – pictures of their special friends, testimonials and presentation objects, Gothic furniture made for Disraeli, his books and writing materials, along with portraits of Queen Victoria. The queen had a special soft spot for 'Dizzy'. In the Church of St Michael and All Angels is the personal memorial she dedicated: 'To the dear and honoured memory of Benjamin Earl of Beaconsfield, this memorial is placed by his grateful Sovereign and friend, Victoria R.I. – "Kings loveth him that speaketh right", Proverbs XVI, 13. February 27 1882'. Benjamin and Mary Anne lie outside the east end of the church, together with Disraeli's brothers and nephew, and a female fan who had begged to be buried beside her hero. There are many other treasures in the church – they include very fine Victorian stained glass, a beautiful early Norman tub font with floral carving, and a calm and blissful Arts and Crafts mural of the Adoration. There is also a curious collection of Tudor forgeries of 13th- and 14th-century knightly tomb effigies; these were installed during the reign of King Henry VIII by local squire George Wellesbourne, in order to give himself a grand set of 'ancestors' and bolster his spurious claim to be descended from the noble De Montfort family.

After visiting Hughenden Manor (861953) return down the drive to the cattle grid above the church (863955). Turn right here and walk south through the park along the valley side, aiming to go through a kissing gate halfway down the fence ahead. From here the path drops gradually down the slope to go through the next kissing gate just above a small lake (863949). The stream soon bends away left, but keep ahead to a road (864944), where you turn left to cross the A4128 (866943). Climb Green Hill Road through a long S-bend. In ½ mile (0.75km), where the road bends sharp right opposite Brands

Hill Avenue at the top of the hill, turn even sharper right (872946 – FP fingerpost) through beech trees to follow a green lane.

'Secret' Lane into High Wycombe

This is a delightful way to enter High Wycombe, nearly a mile of 'secret' lane that drops south along the valley side into the very centre of the town, hedged and fenced all the way; a lane too narrow for cars, but well used by townspeople on foot.

In 350 yards (350m), as the green lane begins to dip steeply downhill, bear left (871943) on a rising track that soon crosses a road (871942). Keep forward along the lane ('No bicycles' notice), descending for ½ mile (0.75km) to cross a road (868933). Keep ahead down The Greenway; turn left at the bottom to cross the A404 (868931), and continue for 250 yards (250m). Turn right down Albert Street and walk through Duke Street car park to enter High Wycombe Station (870930). If this entrance barrier is closed, cross under the railway through the underpass and turn right to reach the front of the station.

4. BERKHAMSTED COMMON, ASHRIDGE HOUSE & FRITHSDEN BEECHES

When 19th-century noble landowners wanted something, they generally got their way. But Lord Brownlow bit off more than he could chew when he decided to enclose Berkhamsted Common in 1866. The full saga of how he was defeated, and the common saved for public enjoyment, unfolds as you cross this open land above Berkhamsted and take a look at Brownlow's grand mansion, Ashridge House. The return walk brings you among the ancient pollarded trees of Frithsden Beeches, a very rare fragment of a medieval wood pasture.

START AND FINISH:	Berkhamsted Station
LENGTH OF WALK:	6½ miles (10.5km)
OS MAPS:	1:50,000 Landrangers 165, 166; 1:25,000 Explorer 181
TRAVEL:	By rail from London Euston (35 mins); by road – M25 (Jct 20), A41.
FEATURES:	Berkhamsted Castle; Berkhamsted Common; Ashridge House; Frithsden Beeches.
REFRESHMENTS:	Many pubs and cafés in Berkhamsted.

To view narrowboats negotiating the locks of the Grand Union Canal, turn right out of Berkhamsted Station (993082) and the canal bridge is 200 yards (200m) along the road. Return past the station and under the railway line. Berkhamsted Castle (995082) is 50 yards (50m) on your right.

Berkhamsted Castle

This is a site with a special place in British history. Berkhamsted Castle was one of the first to be built after the Norman Conquest. Count Robert Mortmain, William the Conqueror's half-brother, began work on a wooden castle beside the River

Opposite, clockwise: Cricket at Ashridge; the Grand Union Canal at Berkhamsted; the beautiful valley that leads to Berkhamsted Common.

Bulbourne immediately after the victory at Hastings. It was here, in November 1066, that William received the homage of those Saxon nobles who had survived the battle, and gave orders to Bishop Ealdred to prepare to crown him king at Westminster Abbey on the forthcoming Christmas Day.

The castle was rebuilt in flint and stone in the mid-12th century, and was a royal residence until Tudor times. It's this early medieval stonework that you see today; a big oval of broken flint curtain wall, some of it standing up to 20 feet (6m) high, encircling the broad platform of the outer ward, with the green grassy thumb of the inner ward's mound sticking up at the north-east corner. To the south, the railway runs through the outer earthworks and moat, having carried away the main gateway and its defensive barbican during construction – they wouldn't get away with it today!

Return from the castle to the roundabout by the railway bridge, and turn right along Brownlow Road. In 100 yards (100m) the road bends right; continue ahead here for 50 yards (50m). At the left bend keep ahead across a stile (994084 – 'Berkhamsted Common 1' FP fingerpost and yellow arrow) through Berkhamsted Collegiate School's sports field car park. At the end of the tarmac continue along a grassy track; cross a stile, and shortly turn left through a kissing gate (996088 – FP fingerpost), continuing up the slope of the hill with the hedge on your left. At the top of the slope continue along a field track, keeping the hedge on your left. The track soon bends left (993094) to run north-west with a hedge on the left. Pass through the hedge at the far end of the field and bear right (991097 – post with three yellow arrows), heading north-north-east past an old pond among bushes, with a hedge on your right. Follow the hedge into a dip and climb to cross a stile into the woods (993102).

Keep straight ahead on a narrow track through the trees for 150 yards (150m), then turn left along a bridleway (post with blue BW arrows), immediately taking the clearer, left-hand track at a fork. In 300 yards (300m) you join the track from Brickkiln Cottage, seen to your right among the trees. Keep ahead to reach the edge of the trees at gates (992104). Continue to follow the path along the inside edge of the wood. In 300 yards (300m) the path bears right (991107) to cross the shank of the wood and meets a bridleway at the northern edge (992108 – post and blue arrows). Turn left here inside the rim of the wood, with open ground on your right. In 300 yards (300m) the path continues ahead deeper into the wood (991110). In 150 yards (150m), keep ahead at a post ('Ashridge Estate Boundary Trail' arrow, '47' marker and blue arrow), to bear right opposite Coldharbour Farm (989113 – posts with blue arrows) on a curving forest road across a wooded sector of Berkhamsted Common.

Berkhamsted Common, Ashridge House & Frithsden Beeches

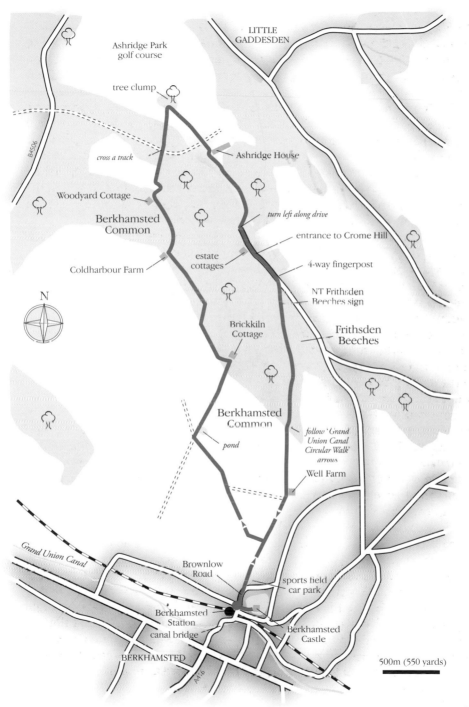

LITTLE
GADDESDEN

Ashridge Park
golf course

tree clump

B4506

cross a track

Ashridge House

Woodyard Cottage

Berkhamsted
Common

turn left along drive

entrance to Crome Hill

estate
cottages

4-way fingerpost

Coldharbour Farm

NT Frithsden
Beeches sign

N

Frithsden
Beeches

Brickkiln
Cottage

Berkhamsted
Common

*follow 'Grand
Union Canal
Circular Walk'
arrows*

pond

Well Farm

Grand Union Canal

Brownlow
Road

sports field
car park

Berkhamsted
Station
canal bridge

Berkhamsted
Castle

BERKHAMSTED

A416

500m (550 yards)

The Battle of Berkhamsted Common

The long tract of open and wooded country along the ridge north of Berkhamsted is a remnant of what was once an enormous common wood called The Frith – 'a wood for a thousand swine' records the Domesday Book. The Frith was a forest where the locals grazed their cattle and cut bracken for fuel and bedding. At prescribed intervals the bounds would be ceremonially beaten and boys bumped at important points to ensure the next generation remembered just where the common's boundaries lay. Berkhamsted residents took for granted their right to roam on the common until 1866, when Lord Brownlow of the adjacent Ashridge Estate arbitrarily enclosed one-third of the ground inside iron fences with no gates or means of access. He had offered the townsfolk 43 acres (17ha) of land in Berkhamsted for a recreation ground in exchange for their rights of commonage, and most had agreed, Esau-like, to take this mess of pottage in exchange for their birthrights. But local property-owner Augustus Smith was determined not to let the peer have his way.

Ironically, Smith himself was a fabulously autocratic landowner who had bought the Scilly Isles and ran them with a rigid rod of iron. But Brownlow's arrogance had got his goat. With the bit of righteousness between his teeth, Smith went into action to rescue Berkhamsted Common from the noble lord's clutches. He organised and paid a gang of navvies to come down from London and remove the iron railings by force. A special train left Euston Station just after midnight, carrying 100 selected men armed with hammers, chisels and crowbars. The two contractors who had engaged them had got blind drunk in a pub near Euston, but a clear-headed lawyer's clerk coordinated the men when they disembarked at Tring Station and marched them up to the common. *Punch* magazine, a fortnight after the event, set the scene:

Spoke out their nameless leader,
'That railing must go down.'
Then firmer grasped the crowbar
Those hands so strong and brown.
They march against the railing,
They lay the crowbars low,
And down and down for many a yard
The costly railings go.

Before first light the men had knocked down 3 miles (5km) of iron railings that had cost Lord Brownlow £1,000 to erect. The railings were neatly rolled up and left for the Ashridge estate workers to collect. In the morning the locals came flocking on foot and in carriages, gigs and dog carts to stroll across the common. Many took away sprigs of gorse as tokens that the land was theirs again.

The National Trust owns most of the common now, and people are free to walk where they will (although certain areas, such as Frithsden Beeches – see below – need to be treated with sensitivity). The Battle of Berkhamsted Common, and other contemporary attempts to enclose Wimbledon Common and Hampstead Heath, had long-term repercussions, leading to the formation of the Commons, Open Spaces and Footpaths Preservation Society, and to a general appreciation of the necessity to preserve such precious open spaces. As *Punch* summed it all up:

Bold was the deed and English
The Commoners have done,
Let's hope the law of England, too,
Will smile upon their fun.
For our few remaining Commons
Must not be seized or sold,
Nor Lords forget they do not live
In the bad days of old.

By Woodyard Cottage (987117) follow the track round a right bend; then turn left over a stile (yellow arrow). Cross the field northwards, passing an arrow on a post, to the angle of a wood, then ahead to cross a stile into the wood (988120). Keep ahead, following white arrows on tree trunks. In 150 yards (150m) cross a track (yellow arrow and 'No Horses' notice). Continue ahead, following white arrows, to leave the wood on the edge of Ashridge Park golf course (989124). Head due north across the fairway (yellow arrow; beware of flying golf balls!) to a tree clump, then turn right and follow a line of white posts to a yellow arrow on a post at the corner of a wood. This arrow points forward through the trees. In 150 yards (150m) leave the trees, with Ashridge House (994122) dead ahead.

Ashridge House

This enormous and imposing mansion (now a college) stands on a monastic site and was remodelled by James Wyatt for the 7th Earl of Bridgewater in 1808 as a Gothic extravaganza. Turrets, chapel spire, battlements and other embellishments reflect the family's wealth, power and prestige – as does the sheer size of the frontage, which is a mighty 1,000 feet (300m) wide. From the edge of the trees you can look back west along a straight avenue 1½ miles (2.5km) long, to see the tall obelisk of the Bridgewater Monument, which was erected in 1832 in memory of the 3rd Duke of Bridgewater, a formidable promoter and builder of canals.

Aim for the right side of Ashridge House to cross a road and turn right (FP fingerpost) along a fence and hedge. In 100 yards (100m) turn left (991121 – a yellow arrow points ahead, but you turn left!) along Ashridge House's boundary fence. Shortly after the buildings end, bear slightly right away from the fence to turn left along the college's drive (995115). Pass Berkhampstead Lodge on the right and the entrance to Crome Hill on the left. In 300 yards (300m) you come to a four-way fingerpost on your left (998110). Two of its 'BW' signs point into the woods on the right of the road. Follow the left-hand of these, slanting uphill for 100 yards (100m), to leave the trees and bear left along the wood edge. In 150 yards (150m), at a 'NT Frithsden Beeches' sign (998108), join a track along the upper edge of the wood. In 200 yards (200m), where the wood edge curves to the right, keep ahead (BW fingerpost) through the woodland of Frithsden Beeches.

Frithsden Beeches

These ancient beech woods, the remains of medieval wood pastures, were acquired by the National Trust in 1925 after the Ashridge Estate had decided to fell them. The oldest beeches are pollards – trees whose limbs have been periodically cut back over the centuries to give clearance for animals to graze. The pollards, some of which could be 250 years old or more, are thick, gnarled trees whose contorted limbs taper up to 60 or 70 feet (18 or 21m). Dead tree limbs lie everywhere, left to rot for the benefit of the insect and bird population. Although the public has unrestricted access to Frithsden Beeches, the NT appreciates it if you keep to the paths in order not to disturb the wildlife of these woods.

In 300 yards (300m) you dip into a dell (blue arrows on a post). Keep ahead, up the slope and on, to leave the trees (999103) and continue south across the scrubland of Berkhamsted Common, crossing several bridleways. Where the scrub trees end, follow 'Grand Union Canal Circular Walk' arrows on posts down a grassy slope and through another belt of woodland. At the bottom edge of the trees, cross a stile (998097) and bear left along a field edge to cross a stile into a hedged, grassy lane. It leads south for $\frac{1}{3}$ mile (0.5km) to Well Farm. Cross a stile here (998092) and follow the field edge back to Berkhamsted.

5. LITTLE CHALFONT TO LATIMER, CHURCH END & CHENIES

Arriving at Little Chalfont by tube, within a few minutes you find yourself exploring the beautiful valley of the River Chess: Latimer village, as pretty as a picture round its green. Take a stroll through the meadows, past the lonely tomb of a most independent-minded brick maker, to a tiny medieval church with wall paintings that are 600 years old. More riverside ramblings bring you back to the tube station by way of one of England's finest Tudor houses, and probably the most striking collection of memorial tombs anywhere in the country.

START AND FINISH:	Chalfont and Latimer tube station (Metropolitan line)
LENGTH OF WALK:	7 miles (11km)
OS MAPS:	1:50,000 Landranger 176; 1:25,000 Explorer 172
TRAVEL:	By tube from central London (50 mins approx.); by road – M25 to Jct 18, A404 to Little Chalfont, car park at tube station.
FEATURES:	Latimer village; tomb of William and Alice Liberty; Holy Cross Church, Church End; Chenies Manor; St Michael's Church, Chenies.
REFRESHMENTS:	Cock Inn, Church End.

From Platform 2 at Chalfont and Latimer tube station (997975), leave the station. Turn right down the approach road and turn sharp left along Bedford Avenue, then first right in 250 yards (250m) up Chenies Avenue (996976). Cross Elizabeth Avenue and continue forwards to where Chenies Avenue bends left into Beechwood Avenue (996981). Walk ahead here down a gravelly path and bear right into the woods. Keep ahead as the path crosses a bridleway and leads downhill. It crosses a broad lower path and continues down to the edge of the wood. From here on, follow blue trout waymarks. Walk down across a field with a view ahead over Latimer Park Farm. The multiple chimneys and gables of Latimer House dominate the slope opposite. Cross the road (999985) and the field beyond, then the bridge over the River Chess, stopping here to enjoy this delectable stretch of English countryside where great horse chestnut, silver birch and plane trees stand along the river that flows down its quiet valley through beds of watercress – an ordered, landscaped slice of rural heaven. Then turn right through a kissing gate and walk beside the river through another kissing gate on to a road (003988), where you turn left to reach Latimer village green.

Latimer

Charming old brick-and-timber cottages surround the little triangular green, where three items catch the eye: the village pump under a tiled pagoda roof; the obelisk memorial to local men who served in the Boer War; and the cairn commemorating Villebois, the favourite horse of the French General de Villebois Mareuil who was killed at the Battle of Boshof on 5 April 1900, in the act of saving the life of Charles Compton Cavendish, Lord Chesham. The grateful Lord Chesham had Villebois

(the horse) brought back to England to end his days in peace and quiet at Latimer. When Villebois died in 1911 the English nobleman had the horse's heart buried here on the green, along with his harness and ceremonial trappings.

Lord Chesham's red-brick mansion, Latimer House, stands just up the road (000989). Rebuilt in Gothic style for the Cavendish family in the mid-19th century after a fire, it's now a conference centre.

Retrace your steps (take care!) from the village green along the road for 50 yards (50m) and turn left over a stile (Chess Valley Walk sign). Follow a path through the fields (trout waymarks) that soon passes above a tangled copse hiding the remnants of Flaunden Old Church (009987).

Mr Liberty the Brickmaker

The few remnants of the flint walls of the medieval church are smothered in bushes and nettles at the nearest corner of the trees. It was left to fall down when a new church was built 1 mile (1.6km) to the north on higher, less flood-prone ground. The old church was anathema in its operative days to at least one freethinking local craftsman. Just above the church ruins you pass the modest brick-built tomb where 'Mr William Liberty of Chorleywood, Brickmaker' lies buried with his wife Alice. Mr Liberty (what more apposite surname could he have

Opposite above: Chenies Manor and Church, seat of the Dukes of Bedford.
Opposite below: Flowery fields beside the River Chess near Latimer.

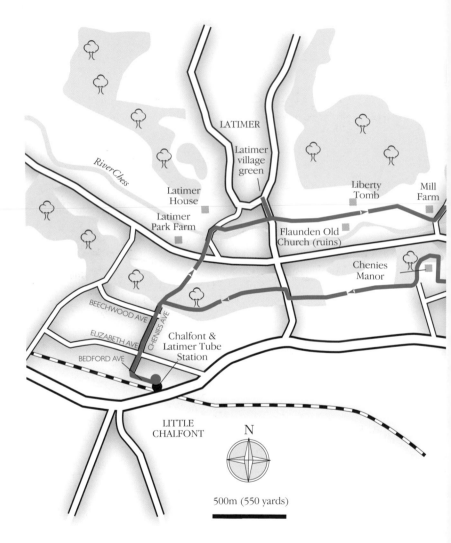

LATIMER

River Chess

Latimer village green

Latimer House

Latimer Park Farm

Liberty Tomb

Mill Farm

Flaunden Old Church (ruins)

Chenies Manor

BEECHWOOD AVE

CHENIES AVE

ELIZABETH AVE

BEDFORD AVE

Chalfont & Latimer Tube Station

LITTLE CHALFONT

N

500m (550 yards)

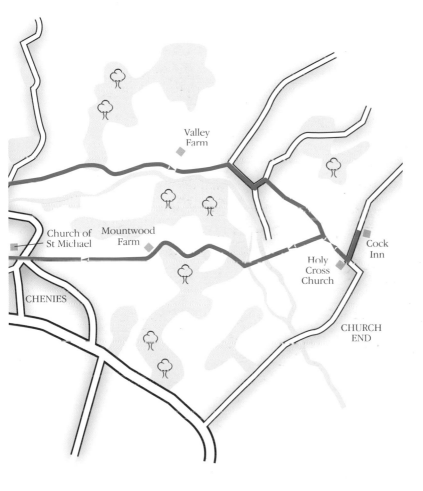

Valley
Farm

Church of   Mountwood
St Michael   Farm

Cock
Inn

Holy
Cross
Church

CHENIES

CHURCH
END

borne?) died in 1777, having stipulated that he should not be laid to rest anywhere within the bounds of the church.

Leave the field and continue ahead along a fenced path, following the trout waymarks for ¹/₃ mile (0.5km) to cross the farmyard of Mill Farm (014988). Turn left up the road for 100 yards (100m), turn right over a stile (Chess Valley Walk sign) and along a fenced track to walk through meadows and woodland.

Chess Valley – Wildflowers and Watercress

The Chess Valley is naturally irrigated by clean water filtered through the underlying chalk. You pass through wildflower meadows, superbly managed by the Chiltern Society, whose watercourses offer refuge to the increasingly rare water vole. Keep an eye out, too, for the watercress farms, where for a couple of pounds you can buy a peppery bunch of locally grown cress to crunch as you walk on.

In ²/₃ mile (1km) you reach the road below Valley Farm (026990). Keep straight ahead down a lane to turn right along a road (031990); follow around a left-hand bend then in 100 yards (100m) turn right over a stile (033990). The sign here is 'Church End 1¹/₂ miles' – in fact it's not much more than ¹/₂ mile (0.75km) across the fields to Holy Cross Church (039984).

Holy Cross Church

The stubby little church, built of flint in the 12th century, its tower capped with Tudor brick and its saddlebacked roof steeply pitched, stands 1 mile (1.6km) south of its parent village of Sarratt. Legend has it that the village had to be shifted to higher ground in the mid-14th century because there were so many plague victims buried around the church. The Cock Inn, a really friendly and delightful country pub just across the road from the church, is reputed to have been built on the unconsecrated ground where hanged felons were buried.

Holy Cross has a cool and beautiful interior where arches of many architectural eras stand under the dark medieval timbers of the roof. On the east wall of the south transept are paintings dating from the 1370s: a slim Virgin with hands raised as Gabriel announces the advent of Christ, a shepherd hurrying to Bethlehem clutching a lamb as an angel blows a double-piped shawm, and a sea of faces below, looking up over a forest of piously folded hands.

Leave the church through the south gate in the churchyard opposite the brick almshouses of 1821 (the Cock Inn is just up the road to the left) and turn right through a kissing gate to reach the valley bottom (035981). Turn right over a stile here and cross a field to the next stile (033984). Turn left here, crossing the River Chess and a second (sometimes dry) stream to reach a junction of paths (032984). Do not take the path ahead through the woods; instead, take the left path via a stile to leave the wood. Cross fields and go along the edge of a wood to join a track by Mountwood Farm (025984). In $^1/_2$ mile (0.75km) this concrete track leads to Chenies village.

Chenies

This model estate village was built in the 1850s by the Duke of Bedford, owner of the great Tudor manor house of Chenies that sits among its trees at the western edge of the village (014984). The many tall chimney stacks on the cottages echo those on the master house, owned by the Russell family, Dukes of Bedford, from 1526 until 1954 when it was sold to pay death duties. Before the 17th century, when the Russells moved to Woburn Abbey and Chenies became ruinous, the grand house had played host to England's great and good. In 1542 the lame King Henry VIII is reputed to have spent the night wandering the corridors in search of his wife, Catherine Howard, who was carrying on an affair. His ghost still walks Chenies, dragging its crippled leg.

With crow-stepped gables and intricately twisted tall chimneys, Chenies looms massively over the 15th-century Church of St Michael. Gloomy inside under a heavy Victorian roof, the entire north side of the church was converted in 1556 into what became known as the Bedford Chapel. This was filled during the following four centuries with the grandest of Russell monuments. Among them are: John Russell the 1st Earl (1485–1555); a languidly lounging effigy of the 1st Duke of Bedford (1613–1700); Lord John Russell (1792–1878), the Victorian statesman (twice prime minister); and the 'Flying Duchess' Mary Russell (1865–1937), wife of the 11th Duke, she disappeared on a solo flight from Woburn in 1937, aged 71 and stone deaf.

Cross the village green and walk up the drive past the church. Turn right between the church and Chenies Manor to enter woodland. Bear left just inside, and keep ahead on the path to emerge through a kissing gate on to a stony track. Turn right and follow this track for $^1/_2$ mile (0.75km) until you reach a road (005982). Turn right, then in 50 yards (50m) go left (FP sign) through woodland. In $^1/_2$ mile (0.75km) you reach the top of Chenies Avenue (996981) and drop down to the tube station.

6. HARLINGTON, BUNYAN'S OAK & SHARPENHOE CLAPPERS

The Chiltern Hills, officially at their northernmost outpost on the outer slope of the Dunstable Downs, own a curious detached enclave several miles further north, the sinuously curving chalk rampart of the Sundon Hills. This is the final step down from the 750-foot (230-m) heights of the Chilterns to the Bedfordshire plains some 500 feet (150m) below. The walk begins at Harlington on the edge of Bedfordshire's lowland country of heavy clay, and works its way round to climb to the crest of the hills for an exhilarating ridge tramp with marvellous chalk downland flowers in spring and summer, and spectacular views at any time of year.

START AND FINISH:	Harlington Station
LENGTH OF WALK:	8 miles (13km)
OS MAPS:	1:50,000 Landranger 166; 1:25,000 Explorer 193
TRAVEL:	By rail from London St Pancras (45 min); by road – M1 (Jct 12), A5120 for ½ mile (0.75km), minor road to Harlington.
FEATURES:	Bunyan's Oak; Sharpenhoe Clappers; Sundon Hills.
REFRESHMENTS:	The Lynmore PH, Sharpenhoe.

Come out of Harlington Station (035303) and go right along the pavement and cross the bridge over the railway; then keep ahead to reach Sundon Road by the war memorial. Turn right downhill. At 100 yards (100m) past the Old Sun Inn, opposite No. 62, turn left (037302; FP fingerpost) up a fenced path. Cross a footbridge and aim diagonally right across the field towards a yellow-topped post (YTP) at the far side. Keep ahead for 70 yards (70m), turn left across a footbridge (043302; a post with black arrow) and follow the field edge with a hedge on your right. Follow arrows to reach a lane below Willow Farm (047303). *NB If you want to continue the main walk without taking the Bunyan's Oak detour (below) see * on page 50.*

Bunyan's Oak Detour

Turn left up the lane, pass Willow

Farm and turn left up the driveway. In 20 yards (20m) keep ahead up a grassy path (fingerpost) for ¹/₄ mile (0.4km) to turn right along a road. At a fork in 50 yards (50m) bear right along the Sharpenhoe Road (044308). In 70 yards (70m) bear left on a footpath (FP fingerpost) through the trees. In 50 yards (50m) cross a kissing gate into a field and turn right along the hedge (FP fingerpost). In 30 yards (30m) follow the 'Public Footpath Pulloxhill 2¹/₂' FP sign across the field, aiming for a water tower on the skyline. Pass to the right of a spinney in the valley bottom and look up the slope where you'll see Bunyan's Oak (046313).

Bunyan's Oak and the Great Parable-spinner

Bunyan's Oak is dead, but still enormously impressive: a gnarled, bifurcated, grey skeleton alone on a rise of ground, its knotty limbs spreading outwards and skywards. Bark flakes off it like saurian hide. It commands a superb view across the fields to Sharpenhoe Clappers, a high chalk spur at the north-east extremity of the Sundon Hills. John Bunyan is said to have based the Delectable Mountains in *The Pilgrim's Progress* on these hills, and the view is certainly an inspiring one.

Bunyan was preaching under this oak on 12 November 1660 when he was arrested for sedition. The local magistrate, Francis Wingate JP, committed Bunyan to Bedford jail, and the preacher was shut up there for the next 12 years. In that nervous era, with widespread fear and loathing of the new Nonconformist religions and their practitioners, prison was an inevitable destination for the Bedfordshire tinker's son with his inextinguishable missionary zeal and his fierce independence of mind.

John Bunyan had not been an especially religious-minded youth. Born in 1628 in the village of Elstow just south of Bedford, he followed his father's trade, and loved to sing, dance and play his fiddle. He married a local girl and had four children. But in his twenties Bunyan began to be troubled by deep upheavals of the spirit. John Gifford, a pioneer of the Independent religious movement, inspired him to preach and to write – Bunyan's first book was a demolition of the tenets of another new branch of faith, Quakerism.

His first long spell in jail gave Bunyan the leisure to write several religious tracts. In 1672 there was a Declaration of Indulgence and a slackening of official persecution of Nonconformist sects. Bunyan was released, and took up a full-time calling as a licensed Independent preacher. But four years later the Declaration was revoked and he landed back in prison – only for six months, but during this time he wrote the first part of *The Pilgrim's Progress*. The Delectable Mountains were often in sight of Christian, the fable's hero, during his dangerous journey from the City of Destruction to the Celestial City, and Bunyan in his prison cell must frequently have had this view of the Sundon Hills in mind as he wrote.

The Pilgrim's Progress was published in 1678, with a sequel in 1685. By that time Bunyan had taken to a wandering life as an itinerant preacher. After riding through a rainstorm in August 1688 he caught a chill, and died soon afterwards.

The great parable-spinner would be pleased to see that his namesake oak shelters a small living elder tree; while in front of the dead giant grows a slender oak sapling, planted by Dr David Bellamy in July 1988 to commemorate the tercentenary of John Bunyan's death.

From the Oak retrace your steps to the lane by Willow Farm. (* *NB Main walk continues here.*) At 100 yards (100m) below Willow Farm, turn left across a footbridge and follow the footpath with a hedge on your right. At the end of the field the path curves left. In 50 yards (50m) ignore a post and arrow pointing right; in another 15 yards (15m) turn right across a railed footbridge (051304), then left along a field edge with a hedge on your left. Pass two YTPs. In another 100 yards (100m), on a right bend (053307), ignore a footbridge and two arrows on your left; bear right instead and follow the path for 1/3 mile (0.5km) to a road (055312). Turn right through Sharpenhoe to pass The Lynmore pub. In 150 yards (150m) turn right (fingerpost 'Chiltern Way/CW extension') up the rounded prow of Sharpenhoe Clappers into the trees. A short, steep climb up steps through the trees puts you quickly at the top (066303), where you turn right along the path at the escarpment edge.

Sharpenhoe Clappers

Looking from east to west there are three sections to this wriggling 6-mile (10km) ribbon of chalk escarpment – Smithcombe Hill, Sharpenhoe Clappers and the Sundon Hills. The beech hanger on top of Sharpenhoe Clappers was not planted until the 19th century, so John Bunyan would have known the hills as bald grassy sheep walks. An Iron Age fort clings to the spur, its ditch running across the path in the upper skirt of the wood. The National Trust looks after clearance of hawthorn and elder scrub on the steep escarpment slope, opening up the ground for summer chalk grassland flora that includes rock rose, horseshoe vetch, milkwort, dwarf thistle and fairy flax. The view to the north over many miles of low-lying country is wonderful.

In 1/3 mile (0.5km) keep ahead on a clear track among scrub bushes, then stick to the right-hand edge of an open grassy area on the nape of the downs, ignoring fenced tracks leading off. A yellow arrow on a gatepost (067298) announces that the Bunyan Trail now shares its course with the ancient Icknield

Opposite: Old commons covered in trees are a feature of the Sundon Hills.

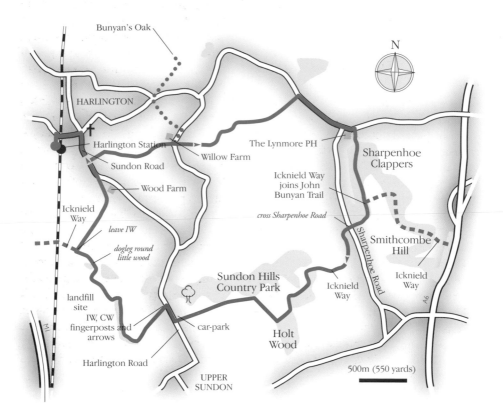

Bunyan's Oak

N

HARLINGTON

Harlington Station

Willow Farm

The Lynmore PH

Sharpenhoe
Clappers

Sundon Road

Wood Farm

Icknield Way
joins John
Bunyan Trail

Icknield
Way

leave IW

cross Sharpenhoe Road

Smithcombe
Hill

*dogleg round
little wood*

Sharpenhoe Road

Sundon Hills
Country Park

Icknield
Way

Icknield
Way

landfill
site

IW, CW
fingerposts and
arrows

car-park

Holt
Wood

A6

M1

Harlington Road

500m (550 yards)

UPPER
SUNDON

Way/IW trackway. Cross Sharpenhoe Road (065296) into an open expanse of upland. A Chiltern Way/CW waymark points you dead ahead to cross the field. At the far side bear left along the fence to go through a kissing gate in the top left corner. Then follow CW waymarks along a fenced path. In the woods ½ mile (0.75km) after crossing Sharpenhoe Road, you reach a post with four arrows (061291). Continue to follow CW, zigzagging along the wood edge for ½ mile (0.75km).

At the west corner of Holt Wood (058285), turn right (CW arrows on a post). Keep the hedge on your right for 300 yards (300m) to go through a kissing gate (056287) and bear left down a track (CW waymark). In another 150 yards (150m) turn left at a gate (BT, IW, CW waymarks) and keep ahead with a hedge on your left for 1/2 mile (0.75km).

Sundon Hills Country Park

Looking north over the wooded escarpment of the Sundon Hills there are views across 20 or 30 miles (32 or 50 km) of country. The 93-acre (38ha) country park comprises native ash woodland, patches of hazel and elder scrub with wayfaring trees, areas of grazed downland and abandoned chalk quarries. Yellowhammers, willow warblers and whitethroats sing in the scrub, and on the downland slopes grow common spotted orchid, basil and thyme, restharrow and kidney vetch, salad burnet and woolly thistle. The backs of these hills are rolling, billowy downland, breezy and sunny – beautiful walking from end to end.

At a Sundon Hills Country Park car park (047286), turn right along Harlington Road for 200 yards (200m), then left (IW, CW fingerposts and arrows) along a field edge with a hedge on your left. At the top of the field bear right (043283), soon crossing into the fringe of woodland to continue a clockwise circuit of the sloping valley. At the bottom (north-west) corner (041287) emerge from the trees and bear left, then right along the field edge. Dogleg around a little wood (039290). In 300 yards (300m) an IW post points left, but you keep ahead (037292), turning right with a hedge on your left towards Wood Farm. In 1/3 mile (0.5km), beside the farm, turn left over a stile (040297 – black arrow), making for the nearer end of a conifer hedge. Go over a stile here (black arrow), and follow arrows over stiles and gates, then diagonally across a paddock to reach the road (038301). Turn left to reach Harlington Station.

7. WATTON-AT-STONE, BENINGTON LORDSHIP & SACOMBE

Rural Hertfordshire is the backdrop to this walk: flinty fields under enormous upland skies, farms perched on ridges and fine oak woods. St Peter's Church at Benington boasts a wonderful collection of masonry oddities and two sumptuous medieval tombs, while there are lovely seasonal gardens at Benington Lordship, not to mention an overblown 1830s folly of a mock-Norman gatehouse. Other churches at Little Munden, Sacombe and Watton-on-Stone are worth looking round (for access, see pages 193–4). The long approach drive, extensive parkland and grand gatehouse of Woodhall Park recall an 18th-century era when entrepreneurs, glutted with money made in India, would lay out magnificent estates to their own greater glory.

START AND FINISH:	Watton-at-Stone Station
LENGTH OF WALK:	12 miles (19km)
OS MAPS:	1:50,000 Landranger 166; 1:25,000 Explorers 182, 193, 194
TRAVEL:	By rail from London Moorgate (45–50 mins); by road – M25 (Jct 23), A1 (Jct 6), A1000, then minor roads by Digswell and Burham Green.
FEATURES:	St Peter's Church, Benington; Benington Lordship; Sacombe Park; Woodhall Park.
REFRESHMENTS:	George and Dragon PH, Watton-at-Stone; The Bell PH, Benington; The Boot PH, Dane End.

Opposite: Benington Lordship is set in lovely gardens.

Duck Lane

*bear right across field
(post with blue arrows)*

Benington
Lordship

The Piggery

cross a farm track

BENINGTON

Graves Wood

The Bell PH

GREEN END

St Peter's Church

pump house

join a track

Peartree Cottage

The Boot PH

bear left along Cotton Lane

Little Munden
School

DANE END

hedge

sewage works

cross a farm track

post with
yellow arrows

A602

St Catherine's
Church

WATTON-AT-STONE

SACOMBE

village pump

Woodhall Park
(school)

Sacombebury
Farm

Watton–at–
Stone Station

A602

fenced path

*cross wall by
ladder stile*

gatehouse

Sacombe
House

Watton
Green

St Andrew and St
Mary's Church

Home
Farm

drive to
Woodhall Park

N

Roads Wood

TONWELL

500m (550 yards)

From Watton-at-Stone Station (296192), bear left to cross the railway and continue along the road into Watton-at-Stone, to reach the village street at a mini-roundabout beside the ornate late Victorian village pump (300194).

Bear left along the village street; in 40 yards (40m) turn right down Mill Lane to cross the River Beane. In 70 yards (70m) at a double fingerpost ('Bridleway Blue Hill ½'), turn left to cross a field, keeping a hedge on your left. In ½ mile (0.75km) the track rises up the field to meet the far hedge (298201 – blue arrow on post). Turn left for 50 yards (50m), then right across the A602. A PB fingerpost on the far side points ahead. Keep a hedge on your left and follow the field edge to a gap in the far hedge where you cross a farm track and keep ahead. In 350 yards (350m), where a hedge comes down the slope to your right, turn left up the middle of the field to turn right along a road. In 500 yards (500m) on a right bend, bear left (297216 – BW fingerpost) along Cotton Lane (note – don't take the low road!), a sunken lane and field track, for 1 mile (1.6km). In the bottom of a dip by a little brick pump house, where the track forks, turn left (296228) up a track with telegraph poles to reach the road (295232), where you turn right along the road (take care!) for ⅓ mile (0.5km) into Benington. At Church Green bear left to reach St Peter's Church (297236).

St Peter's Church, Benington

St Peter's is built of knapped (cut) flint, and possesses a tremendous array of carved stone medieval heads, inside and out. There's a weather-beaten statue over the porch, and in the porch's east window two beautiful stained-glass lights: one with daffodils and a gardener's spade and fork commemorating William Eustace Mills (1881–1957), for 25 years rector of Benington; and the other with snowdrops and a painter's palette, brushes and easel in memory of the long-lived Everilda Louise Tindall Mills (1889–1992). Inside are memorial tombs to medieval knights and their ladies, and more intriguing carved figures, several in exotic headgear. Supporting the chancel arch are two Green Men of contrasting type; nearby there's an imp literally pulling a face. The elaborate ogee arch over the memorial tomb in the chancel carries a couple of gurning heads, and on the reverse a contorted likeness of a king trying to pluck a sword out of his guts. Some say this is King Edward II, depicted as suffering a death far more dignified than the horrors that were actually inflicted on him with a red-hot poker in Berkeley Castle.

In the vestry under the tower hangs a framed Proclamation of 1860 'for the Encouragement of Piety and Virtue, and for the preventing and punishing of Vice, Profaneness, and Immorality' – a fascinating document, revealing plenty about Victorian attitudes and aspirations.

Benington Lordship

Just along the road on the left are the iron gates that lead to Benington Lordship, a conglomeration of house and castle in a wonderfully eccentric mixture of architectural styles. The Lordship is based around the scanty ruin of a Norman stone keep that was built in 1138 by Roger de Valoignes without royal permission. The keep lasted less than 40 years; King Henry II had it destroyed, the Royal Exchequer footing the bill for the hundred picks that were used to carry out the demolition. Various houses were erected on the moated site over the ensuing centuries; the present large red-brick structure was built around 1700, and the twin-towered folly of a gatehouse in 1832. Nowadays Benington Lordship opens its beautiful gardens for a number of short display seasons every year: a summer rose garden, a sunken garden, autumnal shrubbery, a spectacular snowdrop display in late winter and other features.

The village of Benington is centred on a medieval nucleus around the village green, with creaky old houses and cottages – many timber-framed – leaning this way and that. At the foot of Duck Lane there are ducks on the duck pond.

From the gates of Benington Lordship go forward to the T-junction (299237). For refreshment, turn right for The Bell; to continue the walk keep ahead along Duck Lane by the pond ('Bridleway Clay End 1¼, Green End 2½' fingerpost). Beside a house called The Piggery, keep ahead through a squeeze gate. In 400 yards (400m) you reach a post with blue arrows (306241), bear right here to cross two fields along an obvious track (ahead) until you meet and cross a farm track. Turn right for 10 yards (10m) to a junction of farm tracks. Here you'll see two tracks stretching across the fields; take the lower track along the valley bottom, following a watercourse at the bottom of the valley for 1 mile (1.6km), crossing three huge fields. In the final field, the watercourse comes to an end at a bridge/barbed wire. At the top left corner of this field (322225) you cross a junction of tracks and keep ahead up the slope into Graves Wood (324224). After 300 yards (300m) join a track and keep forward to turn right along the road by Peartree Cottage (328223). In 40 yards (40m) leave the road and keep ahead ('Dane End ¾' fingerpost and 'No Horse Riding' notice). Follow the field edge with a hedge on your left. In 300 yards (300m) it bends left (329220 – yellow arrow); in another 300 yards (300m) bear left (two yellow arrows on a post) with trees on your left. Soon the tower and stumpy spire of the church at Little Munden (334219) heave into view. The path leads to a road where you turn right to pass the church and reach Little Munden School on the corner.

Enter a big field to the left of the school and cross diagonally towards Dane End. Go through a kissing gate on the far side to cross a road; keep ahead along a path to cross another road, and ahead again (FP fingerpost) to the village road through Dane End (333214). Turn left here if you want to visit The Boot PH; otherwise turn right along the road and out of Dane End, following it until it crosses a stream by a sewage works. In 250 yards (250m) turn left (332207) across the grass to cross a footbridge and walk up the field edge to a post with yellow arrows. Turn right with a bank on your left and follow it for 3/4 mile (1.25km) to a road (334196). Keep ahead up a rise, and turn left to pass St Catherine's Church, Sacombe (336194). Keep ahead along the track (don't turn left) past a 'Private Road – Keep Out' sign (not applicable to walkers!) to pass Sacombebury Farm (336189) and continue along a drive through Sacombe Park for 1 mile (1.6km).

Sacombe Park

Here the character of the landscape changes. Up to now you have been walking through rolling Hertfordshire farming country, mostly arable, with field surfaces almost more flint than soil, and farmhouses sitting prominently on the clay ridges. But now the walk runs for 3 miles (5km) through the private parkland of Sacombe Park and Woodhall Park, with beautiful open grassland, feature trees and an air of well-manicured orderliness.

Continue along the Sacombe Park drive to reach the A602 (331179). Turn left along the wide grass verge for 250 yards (250m), then cross the road and turn right up the steps ahead and over a stile ('Burrs Green' fingerpost). Go straight along the field edge with a strip of woodland on your right, through the shank of Roads Wood and on to turn right along a road (327179). In 20 yards (20m) turn left ('Ware Road 1/2' fingerpost) down a field edge with a hedge on your left. Continue through a wood, crossing the long drive to Woodhall Park (327182). Leave the trees and follow the wall on your left, to cross it by a ladder stile (326185). Leave the wall to continue directly forward by a yellow arrow on a pole to cross a stile and turn right along the Woodhall Park drive (321184), admiring the clock and cupola on the gatehouse of the mansion.

Woodhall Park

Woodhall Park (318185), now a school, was built around 1777 for Sir Thomas Rumbold, who had made his money serving the East India Company in whatever ways he could – probably none too scrupulously. He died in 1791, and the park was bought by another East India Company nabob, Paul Benfield, who had already been dismissed twice, suspended twice and investigated by the company. Eventually dismissed for good, Benfield was forced to take anything that came his way – it turned out to be a cool £0.5 million, a golden kiss-off from the East India Company. After retirement, Benfield speculated wildly in the City, and got himself elected MP for Shaftesbury – in those days a fabulously expensive operation. By

1805 he was broke, and had to sell Woodhall Park to meet his debts. He fled across the English Channel and died a lonely pauper in Paris in 1810.

Don't go as far as the gatehouse ahead; instead follow the drive as it bends left. Pass Home Farm, then turn left over a brick bridge to reach the A119 (314183). Cross the road (take care!) and go up the drive opposite, past the 'Strictly Private' notice. In 70 yards (70m) branch right off the drive (yellow arrow) and walk diagonally right across an open field. At the far side cross a stile (307184 – yellow arrow); continue through the trees, then on across the following field. At the far side cross a stile (303186) and bear right along a lane to meet the road in Watton Green.

Turn right along the road in Watton Green to St Andrew and St Mary's Church (302189), a fine flint-built church haunted by a Grey Lady who puts in an appearance twice a year. She threw herself off the church tower, local stories say, after being cruelly jilted. In front of the church bear left along the road ('Perrywood' sign). In 150 yards (150m) turn right (300190 – FP fingerpost) along a fenced path. Turn left at the top, then bear right to a road. Turn left to Watton-at-Stone Station.

8. NEWPORT, WIDDINGTON & DEBDEN

The north-west corner of Essex is the most appealing part of the county, with a scatter of delightful medieval towns situated on roads and rivers that have brought prosperity through trade and travellers. The countryside is gently undulating clay land, with large flinty fields threaded by plenty of green lanes. Woods and hedges have not been grubbed out hereabouts, so the landscape wears a well-clothed look. Of the three settlements that you'll visit, Newport has several fine old houses and a parish church with a rare and beautiful painted chest; Widdington boasts its huge old Prior's Hall Barn; and Debden's church reveals a range of architectural styles, from ancient to modern. There are deer, owls, monkeys and flamingos at Mole Hall Wildlife Park, and remnants of landscaped parkland around Debden.

START AND FINISH:	Newport Station
LENGTH OF WALK:	9 miles (14km)
OS MAPS:	1:50,000 Landranger 167; 1:25,000 Explorer 195
TRAVEL:	By rail from London Liverpool Street (1 hr approx.); by road – M11 to Jct 9, B1383 to Newport.
FEATURES:	Open country around Waldegraves Farm; Prior's Hall Barn, Widdington; Mole Hall Wildlife Park; Church of St Mary the Virgin and All Saints, Debden; St Mary's Church, Newport; Newport's main street.
REFRESHMENTS:	Fleur-de-Lys PH, Widdington; White Hart PH, Debden; White Horse Inn PH, Newport.

Cross the railway line at Newport Station (522336) to platform 1, and turn right along the lane; after 100 yards (100m) it veers left and climbs as a sunken lane up the left side of a great chalk pit (concrete BW fingerpost). At the top of the sunken lane (529332) keep ahead with a hedge on your left through the fields for ½ mile (0.75km) to a road (536329). Bear left for 100 yards (100m); then at the left bend keep ahead ('Waldegraves Farm' sign) up a farm track, passing Waldegraves Farm and barns (538329). Waldegraves Farm is a nice old house, and the weatherboarded walls of its barns conceal much older frameworks of crooked, ancient timbers that were only roughly dressed by the carpenters before being erected. Follow the track across the middle of a field.

Around Waldegraves Farm

Looking around as you walk through these big upland fields, you'll get a roof-of-the-world feeling. This is open, airy country, well wooded and hedged, with sticky reddish clay in the fields. Map names tickle the fancy: Hanging Grove, Pig's Parlour, Cabbage Wood, London Jock Wood.

At the west corner of Cabbage Wood (544327), the bridleway continues ahead; but turn right here (concrete FP fingerpost and yellow arrow) across a field and down the right side of Park Wood. Cross a footbridge (543322) and follow the path across a field to the edge of some trees with houses behind them (541319). Turn right along the copse edge (yellow arrow). In the corner of the field turn left beside St Mary the Virgin Church; bear right around the church to reach the road at Widdington village green (538317). Turn right for ¼ mile (0.4km), then left (brown 'Prior's Hall Barn' sign) to reach Prior's Hall Barn (537317).

Prior's Hall Barn

This magnificent medieval barn forms part of a working farmyard. Other, lesser buildings stand nearby, so its full effect only hits home when you are standing inside this 'Cathedral of the Harvest', with its almost cathedral-like proportions: 124 feet (33m) long, and 38 feet (11.5m) high. At one end stands the old raised threshing stage, its planking full of gaps. Gnarled oak timbers soar into the shadowy roof, to sprout side shoots and curved supporting arms. Prior's Hall Barn is a north-west Essex aisled barn of crown post and collar purlin construction, say the architects. It was long thought to be of late 14th-century date; but dendrochronology (dating of its timbers), and the records of New College, Oxford, who originally ordered its construction on what was one of their Essex estates, have fixed it pretty firmly to 1440–42.

New College sold the barn to the Prior's Hall farmer in 1920. Up until 1976 it was still used for storing grain and straw, and must have been a splendid site when full to the rafters. It had to be re-roofed during its restoration in 1977–83, using acres of red Sussex tiles. The original structure consumed 400 oaks, and it may not be too fanciful to say that there is something green and forest-like attached to this great barn's atmosphere.

Opposite: The carved base of the oriel window at Monk's Barn in Newport's main street shows the Coronation of the Blessed Virgin Mary. The Mother and Child are flanked by angels playing a harp and a pair of organs.

From the barn, return to Widdington village green. The village sign, erected in honour of the Millennium, shows Prior's Hall Barn, with a brown-habited monk scything corn and another gathering the stooks. Continue past the green and the Fleur-de-Lys pub; in 100 yards (100m) turn left along Cornells Lane ('Wildlife Park' sign). Ignore the first two fingerposts (pointing left, then right, respectively) and in ¼ mile (0.4km) turn left through the hedge (541314) at a double fingerpost. Take the right-hand of the two paths, aiming diagonally right across a field for trees on the far side. Turn right and walk along the field edge to meet a road (547315).

Mole Hall Wildlife Park

If you want to visit the wildlife park, turn right along the road to Cornell's Lane; turn left here, then in 120 yards (120m) left again ('car park' sign) into the grounds of Mole Hall. This wildlife park displays beasts and birds in an agreeable jumble: fallow, sika and red deer; otters and wild cats; wallabies and llama-like guanacos; monkeys and lemurs; cranes and flamingos. There are plenty of cuddly rabbits and guinea pigs, too. The house of Mole Hall is a wonderful early medieval hall on a moated site.

Back where the field path meets the road (547315), keep forward along the lane past Swayne's Hall entrance. Pass Mole Hall Farm, and continue along a green lane. In 40 yards (40m) a FP fingerpost points left; but keep straight ahead here on a green lane, which starts between hedges and then emerges to run along field edges. Continue ahead along this path, following the blue bridleway signs. In ¾ mile (1.25km) the hedge turns right; but keep ahead, following a blue 'bridleway' arrow on a post pointing ahead across a short tract of field to a path between hedges. Follow this path, and in another 120 yards (120m) you'll see a post with public byway markers (orange) where the path meets a gravelly track (559319). Follow the left marker here, with a wood and then a hedge on your left. Soon you enter a green lane, which leads north to Rook End Lane (557325). Turn right for 50 yards (50m) to the gate of a sewage works (fingerpost), then left along a fenced path that skirts the works. Keep ahead up a field to walk down the right side of Brocton's Plantation. At the end of the wood keep ahead with a hedge on your right to reach the road in Debden opposite the White Hart pub (556334). Turn left; in 50 yards (50m), on a sharp right bend, keep ahead ('Parish Church' sign) down a lane for ¼ mile (0.4km) to reach Debden church (551332).

Church of St Mary the Virgin and All Saints, Debden

The 13th-century Church of St Mary the Virgin and All Saints is a curious mixture of architectural styles. The main body of the church has round Norman-looking pillars and gently pointed arches to the wide arcades. Up five steps there's a raised 18th-century

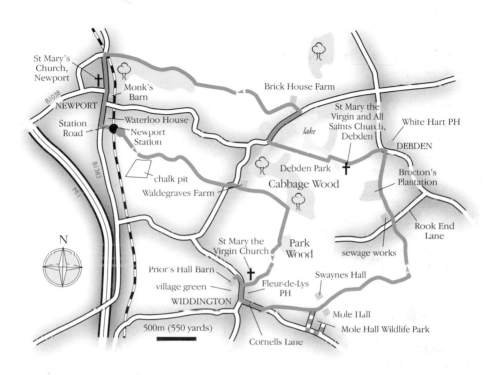

St Mary's Church, Newport

Monk's Barn

NEWPORT

Station Road

Waterloo House

Newport Station

chalk pit

Waldegraves Farm

Brick House Farm

St Mary the Virgin and All Saints Church, Debden

White Hart PH

DEBDEN

lake

Debden Park

Cabbage Wood

Brocton's Plantation

Rook End Lane

N

St Mary the Virgin Church

Park Wood

sewage works

Prior's Hall Barn

village green

WIDDINGTON

Fleur-de-Lys PH

Swaynes Hall

Mole Hall

Mole Hall Wildlife Park

500m (550 yards)

Cornells Lane

chancel with an elaborate Moorish ceiling. At the north-east corner of the church a new late 20th-century brick extension, complete with pinnacles, has been tacked on. The west end of the church supports a stumpy weatherboarded bell turret topped with a fine Essex broach spire.

A stained-glass window inside the church displays the armorial devices of local families. A dove with an olive bough in its beak belongs to the Chiswells; a winged Star of David represents the Muilman clan; and the Trench family is signified by an arm upraised with its hand clutching a dagger. St Mary's is, frankly, a bit of a stylistic porridge, but one that is full of character. Its situation among dark yews in the bottom of a dell is striking, too, and lends the church a slightly sinister air.

You can choose the path that crosses the churchyard, or the one that runs around its perimeter. On the west side the path continues, bending to the left to cross an outlying limb of the great lake in Debden Park (549333). Keep ahead for 50 yards (50m); then turn right (FP sign) to cross two fields. Debden Hall, a handsome Georgian country house, was demolished in 1936; its extensive parkland still survives, centred on the great curved lake. You can catch glimpses of this to your right as you move west through the fields.

At a road at the left corner of a wood (541335) turn right. Keep to the grass verge of the road for ¹/₃ mile (0.5km). Cross a stream, then in 150 yards (150m) turn left through Brick House Farm gate (545338). Follow the left-hand of two FP fingerposts along a driveway below the farm. Pass a house, cross a stile, then follow the leftward curve of the valley. Keep the fence on your right as the valley swings west-south-west, then north-west and then west. In ³/₄ mile (1.25km) you enter woods at a stile (534341 – yellow arrow); then emerge again to keep ahead along the valley bottom. Go under the railway (522345) to reach the B1383 in Newport, where you turn left along the main street. In ¹/₄ mile (0.4km) cross the street and turn right up Wicken Road; walk up the sloping footpath and turn right along Church Street to St Mary's Church (521341).

St Mary's Church, Newport

Newport's church is a fine and elaborate flint structure with a great collection of strange gargoyles, more Eastern than European in inspiration: a lion, a monkey, a be-turbaned sage, a masked devil, and a Buddha-like figure with two cheeky little faces peeping out from the shelter of its jowls. The interior, tall and light, has some beautiful old stained glass in a pair of lancet windows in the west wall of the north transept. The top and bottom panels are a jumble of odd fragments, but each centre panel contains a coherent figure: St Katherine and her wheel of torture on the left and on the right a partly armoured figure supporting a shield with a red cross – perhaps St George.

The chief treasure of the church, however, is the 13th-century altar chest in the south transept, its painted lid propped open as a reredos. A crucified Christ, his legs drawn up, is flanked by his mother and St John, their upper torsos drawn back in conventional but expressive attitudes of pain and horror, their mouths downturned. The artistry is direct but subtle, perfect in its simplicity.

Newport

Back on the main street, turn right and continue to walk along. On the left you'll find the 15th-century Monk's Barn, with many oak studs filled in with herringbone-pattern brickwork. One projecting window has a carved beam, rather eroded by weather, on which you can make out a religious scene: the Coronation of the Virgin Mary. She sits grasping a sceptre with a curly-haired Jesus on her left hand, while angels hymn her from both sides with musical instruments – a pipe organ and a harp.

There are handsome brick Georgian buildings along the street, and striking oversailing black-and-white gables in the Old Vicarage. Above the shop window of Waterloo House (est. 1687) sits a bust of a Civil War personage with curly moustaches and an armoured collar and throat guard. It could be Oliver Cromwell, but is more likely to represent King Charles I. The King was at Newport when Sir Harbottle Grimston of Colchester made a dramatic petition, kneeling while he pleaded for Charles to come to a peaceful accommodation with Parliament and prevent yet more bloodshed. But the king refused to listen, preferring to continue down the path that led eventually to his own execution in 1649.

At the foot of the town, turn left along Station Road to reach Newport Station.

9. KELVEDON, COGGESHALL & FEERING

From Kelvedon you walk out through gentle Essex farming countryside, passing tranquil Pointwell Mill to stroll beside the River Blackwater up to Coggeshall Abbey. In the beautiful little town of Coggeshall there is a wealth of medieval building to admire – notably the ancient Grange Barn, and the richly carved wool-merchant's house of Paycocke's – before setting back south across the fields. All Saints at Feering is a wonderful church, with several medieval treasures. And don't forget to leave enough time, before catching your train, to explore the handsome houses along Kelvedon's long main street.

START AND FINISH:	Kelvedon Station
LENGTH OF WALK:	7½ miles (12 km)
OS MAPS:	1:50,000 Landranger 168, 1:25,000 Explorers 183, 195
TRAVEL:	By rail from London Liverpool Street (50 mins); by road – M25 (Jct 28), A12.
FEATURES:	Pointwell Mill; Coggeshall Abbey buildings; Grange Barn; Paycocke's, Church of St Peter-ad-Vincula, Woolpack Inn and many buildings at Coggeshall; All Saints Church, Feering.
REFRESHMENTS:	The Woolpack and Chapel Inn, Coggeshall; Bell Inn, Feering.

Kelvedon

Kelvedon is a pleasant little town straggling out along what was the main road from Colchester to London before the A12 bypass was built. Looking down the straight line of the street, it's no surprise to learn that this was a Roman road. The Romans knew Kelvedon as Canonium. They built their town on the site of a Belgic village, with the River Blackwater guaranteeing a constant supply of water. The river wriggles under a bridge not far from the railway station, and cradles the south part of the town. The High Street is lined

Opposite: Dark and cosy, The Woolpack makes a characterful lunch stop in Coggeshall.

with 18th-century houses, and plenty of much older ones too, all very easy on the eye.

If you want to explore Kelvedon's High Street straight away, turn right out of the station car park (863193). To start the walk, however, turn left from the station main entrance along the road. At the first left bend, turn right through a gate (863195 – FP fingerpost) and keep ahead along the field edge with a willow grove and the River Blackwater on your right. At the end of the first field, aim diagonally left across the next field (yellow arrow) to go through a gap in the hedge. Follow the line of an old field boundary that bisects the field, keeping ahead to the skyline (862203). Here you join a lane for $\frac{1}{2}$ mile (0.75km), passing Coggeshall Hall to reach a row of poplars (858210 – yellow arrows on a post). Aim diagonally left across the next field, passing to the right of a big depression to reach the road 200 yards (200m) to the right of a line of cottages (855211 – concrete FP fingerpost). Turn right for an unpleasant but inescapable $\frac{1}{4}$ mile (0.4km) of road, with a grass verge most of the way, into Coggeshall Hamlet. Just past the telephone box, turn right down Pointwell Lane to reach Pointwell Mill (853215).

Pointwell Mill

This is a delightful picture: the old brick-built mill and a bent weatherboarded cottage side by side, fronted by weeping willows and undercut by a sluicing millstream. The cottage could be up to 700 years old, thinks the mill owner – that would make it nearly contemporary with Pointwell's sister mill at Coggeshall Abbey, $\frac{1}{2}$ mile (0.75km) up the River Blackwater.

To reach the abbey mill and buildings on the outskirts of Coggeshall, walk round Pointwell Mill house (yellow arrows on a gatepost and shed wall), over a bridge and through an iron gate, to continue forward along the right bank of the mill stream. Near Coggeshall Abbey the stream divides (855220); follow the right-hand channel until you are opposite the abbey buildings, then turn left over the mill bridge (855222) and through the farmyard beside the ancient Chapel of St Nicholas.

Coggeshall Abbey

Coggeshall Abbey is one of those secluded English spots that stays in the mind as an epitome of peace and time-suspended beauty. On one hand you have the old weatherboarded mill, bowed under its big sloping tiled roofs and tall chimney, half drowned in greenery. On the other stands the handsome pink-washed Elizabethan house that was built on the foundations of Coggeshall Abbey some 50 years after the monastery was shut and destroyed on the orders of King Henry VIII. Protectively surrounding the house are outbuildings and ancillary quarters where you can trace the outlines of cloister arches, doorways, lancet

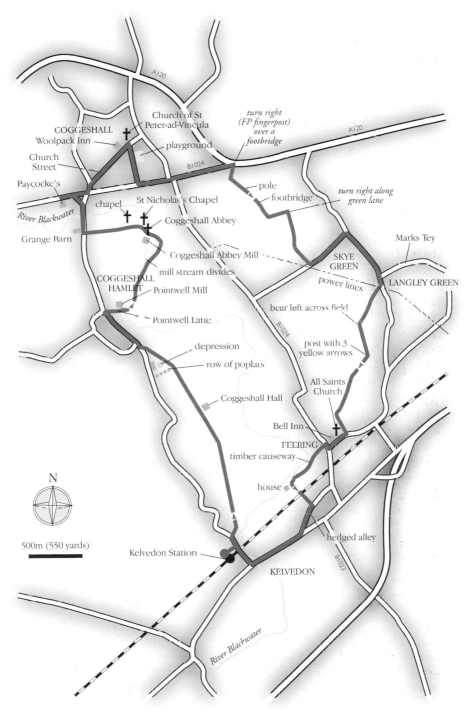

Church of St
Peter-ad-Vincula

turn right
(FP fingerpost)
over a
footbridge

A120

COGGESHALL
Woolpack Inn

playground

B1024

Church
Street

pole

Paycocke's

footbridge

turn right along
green lane

chapel

St Nicholas's Chapel

Coggeshall Abbey

River Blackwater

Marks Tey

Grange Barn

Coggeshall Abbey Mill

**SKYE
GREEN**

mill stream divides

**COGGESHALL
HAMLET**

power lines

LANGLEY GREEN

Pointwell Mill

bear left across field

Pointwell Lane

B1024

depression

post with 3
yellow arrows

row of poplars

All Saints
Church

Coggeshall Hall

Bell Inn

FEERING

timber causeway

N

house

500m (550 yards)

hedged alley

Kelvedon Station

B1023

KELVEDON

River Blackwater

71

windows and sections of wall from the Cistercian abbey founded in the 1140s.

The red-brick Chapel of St Nicholas, with its four brick-framed lancet windows, is a rarity; it was built as the gate chapel of Coggeshall Abbey around 1225, an extraordinarily early date to be using newly made brick. The art of brick and tile making lapsed in Britain for some 800 years after the Romans left around AD 410. Almost all brick building predating the 14th century re-uses Roman materials, so to see building with thicker bricks than the Romans ever employed, evidently made specifically for the construction of this handsome little chapel, is to witness a moment of architectural history established and then frozen in time.

In front of the abbey buildings stand cattle sheds and stables. Cows and horses, hens and ducks, hay bales and fruit orchards – Coggeshall Abbey still has an aura of rural self-sufficiency. From the abbey, walk up Abbey Lane for 1/3 mile (0.5km) and cross straight over the road to find Grange Barn on your left (848222).

Coggeshall Grange Barn

The Grange Barn at Coggeshall is one of Europe's oldest barns – probably the oldest, in fact. This mighty 'Cathedral of the Harvest' is estimated to date back to around 1140, about the same time as the foundation of Coggeshall Abbey. By the late 20th century it was a gap-roofed ruin, far too big for modern farming needs, far too expensive and difficult for one

farmer to keep in repair in an era when the number of men employed around the farm had plummeted. But the Coggeshall Grange Barn Trust was formed by local enthusiasts, and with help from the district and county councils they put it back into tip-top order during the 1980s. It is a highly atmospheric building, with a bare dry forest of timbers rising and spreading to hold up the enormous area of tiles that make up the great barn roof.

From Grange Barn go back to the road and turn left to cross the River Blackwater. Continue along the road to cross a stream by an iron bridge and bear left, then left again along Coggeshall's main street ('Braintree' sign) to find Paycocke's 100 yards (100m) along on the left (848225).

Paycocke's

Paycocke's was built around 1505 by Coggeshall woolman John Paycocke for his clothier son Thomas. It is a magnificent specimen of a nouveau-riche Tudor woolmaster's house, an outward and visible measurement of the householder's wealth in richness of woodcarving and acreage of timber and glass. The silvery wood of the facade timbers is heavily carved. Among the embellishments are a grinning figure bearing a shield embossed with a leering face, a king and queen intimately entwined, a beggar and a priest, a jester in a pointed cap and an upside-down dragon – all these entwined in foliage. There are tall flanking figures to the big carriage doorway and many other enjoyable details to be spotted. Inside the house is a high-ceilinged hall with beautifully carved oak timbers, a dining room with rich linenfold panelling and a fireplace carved with lions, deer and dogs, and a little sitting room where exquisite 19th-century Coggeshall lace is displayed. Upstairs there is more linenfold panelling and ceiling-beam embellishment in the two bedrooms and a fireplace surround carved with a bristle-backed boar, a unicorn and a strange diplodocus-like beast.

Leaving Paycocke's, turn right to return up the street. Opposite the White Hart Hotel turn left, then immediately right along Church Street ('Earl's Colne' sign) for ½ mile (0.75km), to pass the 15th-century Woolpack Inn – beamed, gabled, with crooked walls and charm to burn – and reach the Church of St Peter-ad-Vincula (854230).

Church of St Peter-ad-Vincula, Coggeshall

St Peter's Church was built around the same time as The Woolpack, and beautified by the rich woolmen of Coggeshall. You'll find brasses to the Paycockes in the floor of the north chapel, and on the south chapel wall there is a memorial to the remarkably fecund and long-lived Margaret Honywood. At her death in 1620 she left 367 descendants – 16 children, 164 grandchildren, 228 great-grandchildren and 9 great-great-grandchildren.

From the church, cross the road. Bear left for 30 yards (30m), then right down a path (fingerpost) past a playground. Continue across a playing field to the B1024 (855226). Turn left along the pavement for ½ mile (0.75km) until the road bends left to join the A120. Keep ahead here (862228) along a cul-de-sac road for 50 yards (50m), then turn right (FP fingerpost) over a footbridge. Continue along the field edge for 100 yards (100m). Just past a telephone pole turn left through the hedge (yellow arrow on a post). In the field beyond, aim ahead for the pole in the middle of the field (a pylon is seen beyond and a little to the right). Then follow the direction indicated by a yellow arrow on a pole in the middle of the field, to a gap in the far hedge where you cross a bridge over a ditch (865225). Aim slightly right to a post on the far side of the next field. Turn left (a yellow arrow points right here, confusingly!) along the field edge, to turn right along a bridleway for ⅓ mile (0.5km).

At the end of the lane (870219) turn left along the road, then right at a T-junction ('Feering, Kelvedon' sign). Continue to Langley Green where the road splits (Marks Tey sign); bear right here (876218 – FP fingerpost) along a field edge with a hedge on your left, and under power lines. At the end of the field turn left over a footbridge, then bear right (yellow arrows) with the hedge on your right. In 130 yards (130m) bear diagonally left (874214) across the field, aiming for the left end of the hedge on the far side (post with three yellow arrows). Turn right along the field edge, with the hedge on your right, to go through the corner of the next hedge. Bear diagonally left here (873209 – yellow arrow on post) on a clear path towards Feering church. At the far side of the field turn left, following the fingerpost until you hit the road and turn right to Feering church (872204).

All Saints Church, Feering

All Saints Church has a fine tall Tudor brick porch; its niche holds a modern terracotta bas-relief of the Virgin and Child. Inside you'll find some fascinating old glass in a north window and two alabaster statues from Colne Priory dated to around 1400 – that of the Virgin and Child supported by little censing angels is especially beautiful. In the north or Lady Chapel hangs a *Risen Christ* altarpiece, a replica of that painted by John Constable in 1822. Christ leans back with his arms wide and hands outstretched, a white cloak billowing around him and a fiery sky as a background – a most dramatic depiction.

From the church, pass the Bell Inn to reach the B1024. Turn right, then in 10 yards (10m) turn left through a wicket gate (concrete FP fingerpost and 'No cycling' symbol) along a path. It crosses a bog by a timber causeway, then continues as a grassy path. At a house the path bends left (868200) to run under the railway. In 150 yards (150m) turn right along a hedged alley (870198 – FP fingerpost). At the road (869195) turn right into Kelvedon to return to the station.

10. INGATESTONE, BUTTSBURY & MOUNTNESSING HALL

In the gently rolling farming landscape north-east of Brentwood sits Ingatestone Hall, a superb Tudor mansion built by a poor man's son who made good: he became Privy Councillor to four of the five great Tudor monarchs. The hall forms the centrepiece of this walk, which also takes in a pretty chapel on a ridge, stables and horse paddocks down in the valley of the River Wid, and the handsome house-and-church grouping at Mountnessing Hall.

START AND FINISH: Ingatestone Station

LENGTH OF WALK: 7 miles (11km)

OS MAPS: 1:50,000 Landranger 167 or 177; 1:25,000 Explorer 175

TRAVEL: By rail from London Liverpool Street (35–40 mins); by road – M25 (Jct 28), A12 to Ingatestone.

FEATURES: Ingatestone Hall; Buttsbury Chapel; horse paddocks and stables between Buckwyns Farm and Hannikin's Farm; Mountnessing Hall and Church of St Giles Mountnessing; Westlands Farm and Tilehurst.

REFRESHMENTS: Plenty of pubs and refreshments in Ingatestone.

The architecture of Ingatestone Station (650992) is a fine example of the sensitivity with which the early railway companies had to tread. The Eastern Counties Railway Company must have been well aware, when they were planning their new line from London to Colchester in the 1830s, that Lord Petre of Ingatestone Hall, a powerful and canny figure, owned one of Essex's finest Elizabethan country houses less than a mile from the proposed route of the railway. So the station they provided for Ingatestone when the line opened in 1841 is a brave – and fairly successful – stab at mock-Elizabethan, a red-brick building with diamond patterns inset in dark brick, lattice windows and tall mock-Tudor chimneys. It makes a grand gateway to this walk.

Leaving the station from Platform 2, turn left and follow a footpath parallel to the railway for 200 yards (200m). Then turn left under the railway and along Hall Lane for 400 yards (400m) to a sharp right bend. Turn off the road here, keeping ahead on a footpath for 50 yards (50m); then turn right on another footpath. Just before Ingatestone Hall Farm, yellow arrows on a fence post (653987) give you a choice – left to continue the walk, or right to the gates of Ingatestone Hall.

Ingatestone Hall

Ingatestone Hall (654985) is a really fine Tudor country house, exactly the kind of rambling, extensive domain you would expect a Privy Councillor to possess. Sir William Petre (d. 1572), the founder of his family's fortunes, certainly knew how to seize his chances when they came. He was the son of a tanner from Devonshire and worked his way up, as a bright young Elizabethan lawyer could do in that Golden Age of self-confidence and open opportunities. William eventually served as Secretary of State to King Henry VIII, and was Privy Councillor to no fewer than four Tudor monarchs – Henry and his three offspring, King Edward VI, Queen Mary and Queen Elizabeth I.

In 1535 he was assistant to Thomas Cromwell when King Henry VIII's Chief Secretary was weighing up the wealth of the monasteries prior to their dissolution. Cromwell sent Petre to Essex to list the monasteries' holdings there, and when the young lawyer saw Barking Abbey's manor of Yenge-atte-Stone (Ingatestone) he coveted it on sight and took out a lease on it. The handsome house he built on the site in the 1540s had piped water and flush-through drains, so it was modern and comfortable as well as impressive. Ingatestone Hall has reduced in size over the centuries, but still remains eye-catching with its ranks of mullioned and latticed windows, acres of tiled roofs, crowstepped gables and castellated turrets.

You approach the house through a fine half-timbered gatehouse surmounted by a clock tower. The clock has only one hand, but keeps the hours efficiently as it has done for 250 years. The Petre motto, 'Sans Dieu Rien' – 'Without God, Nothing' – runs round the clock, a suitably pious tag for a family that maintained its Catholic faith throughout the worst phases of persecution in Tudor and Stuart times. Inside the house you can see the cramped, claustrophobic hidey-holes – one in the study, the other in a concealed chamber off the staircase – where evidence of the Petres' illegal adherence to their faith could be hidden if the authorities were about. Catholic priests may have been concealed, but the holes were

Opposite: In Tudor times of religious persecution, many a Catholic priest lived in hiding and in fear of his life among the secret refuges of Ingatestone Hall.

probably for Mass vestments and plate. Priests were certainly welcomed at Ingatestone Hall; they pretended to be members of the household, though a wagging tongue could betray them at any time, as happened to the Jesuit priest John Payne, who was arrested after a fellow servant gave him away. The punishment meted out to Payne – he was hanged, drawn and quartered in public in the market square at Chelmsford in 1582 – hung over the heads of all these brave men, smuggled into England from exile and hidden in great recusant houses like Ingatestone.

Other interesting features of the interior of the hall are the drawing room with its forest of deer antlers on the walls and its rare George Stubbs portraits of the 9th and the 10th Lord Petre; the dining room with fine linenfold oaken panelling and a splendidly vigorous tapestry depicting St George efficiently despatching the dragon with sword and lance; and the 95 feet- (29m-) long gallery hung with portraits of the family, including a wise and rather cagey-looking Sir William, builder of the house. Anyone who managed to retain his Catholic faith, and his head, while serving four monarchs with opinions as divergent and fiercely held as those of the Tudors, must have been exceptionally crafty.

From Ingatestone Hall return to the post with yellow arrows just above the farm (653987). Walk ahead along the side of the hall grounds, with good views of its roofs, turrets and chimneys. Follow yellow arrow waymarks through the fields. This is real Essex farming countryside of wide fields with spreading hedge oaks and rocket-shaped poplars casting long shadows under big skies. Note that some of the footbridges across the watercourses have knee-high bars to negotiate – these are to block the bridge to sheep, not to you! In ½ mile (0.75km), cross the left hand of two adjacent footbridges over the River Wid (661987); follow the river bank to the right, then aim ahead to Buttsbury Chapel on its ridge (664986).

Buttsbury Chapel

This 14th-century chapel, sheltered among its trees, has the beauty of simplicity. Its weatherboarded bell turret is crowned by a bell finial. The north door has enormous, elaborate curly iron hinges. Graffiti of the 18th and 19th centuries is incised around the doorway in the weatherboarded south porch. Inside, a wall tablet pays a movingly direct tribute to Edward Freeman Hudson (1906–89), '50 years a Clerk in Holy Orders, Vicar of the Parish from 1952 to 1988: A loving Priest and true friend to all'.

From the chapel bear right down the road named Buttsbury. Pass a house on the left, and at the next field hedge on the left cross a footbridge and stile (662982). Aim diagonally left across the field; cross another footbridge and follow the path along the hedge and through Little Farm, crossing stiles. Continue through a

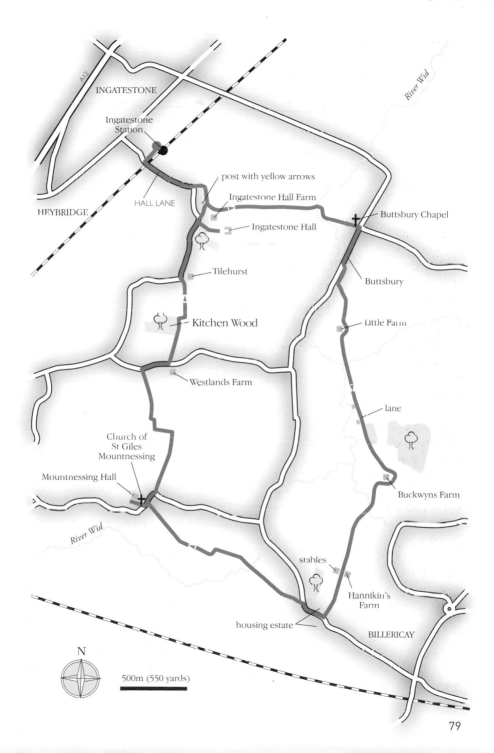

INGATESTONE

Ingatestone
Station

post with yellow arrows

Ingatestone Hall Farm

HALL LANE

HEYBRIDGE

Ingatestone Hall

Buttsbury Chapel

Tilehurst

Buttsbury

Kitchen Wood

Little Farm

Westlands Farm

lane

Church of
St Giles
Mountnessing

Mountnessing Hall

Buckwyns Farm

River Wid

stables

Hannikin's
Farm

housing estate

BILLERICAY

N

500m (550 yards)

River Wid

paddock with a fence on your right to meet the River Wid in the valley bottom (663976). Note – this working farm can be extremely muddy, especially after wet weather. Cross a small tributary that runs into the river here and follow the river (keeping it on your right) up to a fence. Turn left at the fence, and in 50 yards (50m) cross a stile in the hedge into a shady lane. At the end of the lane, cross a road and go over a stile (664970 – 'Public footpath 183 to Buckwyns' fingerpost), passing through scrubby trees to cross a fence (yellow arrow) and keep ahead up a lane and then the drive of Buckwyns Farm (666968). Just before the house, the path swings left (yellow arrow), clockwise around the house. Ignore a bridleway fingerpost on your left and continue clockwise, making three sides of a square around the house. On the far side (665967 – south-west corner), yellow arrows direct you right along a fence, to leave the field over two stiles. Follow signs to the left, with a hedge on your left, down to cross a footbridge; then keep ahead over a stile and cross a field, to walk south-south-west for ¹/₂ mile (0.75km), between a paddock fence and a hedge, and through Hannikin's Farm stable yard (663961).

Horse Country

The lanes that thread this lush, dampish valley bottom are overhung with hazel and lime trees. There are tangled old orchards, and patches overgrown with stubby oaks like damp commons. The green meadows have been fenced off to make paddocks, and in the fields between Buckwyns Farm and Hannikin's Farm (two fine medieval yeoman's names) you'll see plenty of horses grazing. At Hannikin's the inmates of the stables may look out over their half-doors. There's a wild, slightly anarchic feel to these rather ramshackle farms and small horse businesses, in contrast to the neat, house-proud estates of north Billericay into whose outskirts you now walk.

The gate out of Hannikin's Farm stable yard has no signs or waymarks, but keep ahead. At the end of the lane (662958) keep ahead through a housing estate. In 100 yards (100m) you reach a T-junction and turn right along the road. In 150 yards (150m), at a right-hand bend, go left (660958 – 'Footpath 199' fingerpost) and keep forward between the field edge and a fence. After three fields, cross the River Wid on a footbridge (656961) and aim ahead to the left of a house. Cross a stile over a fence; then continue, to cross a stile into a lane (653962). Turn left; in 10 yards (10m) go right through the hedge and over a footbridge. Keep ahead across the fields, aiming just to the left of Mountnessing's church spire. Cross a stile and the road to reach the church (648966).

Church of St Giles Mountnessing and Mountnessing Hall

The Church of St Giles Mountnessing makes a compact huddle – a low brick chancel, a taller flint nave butted up close, and a weatherboarded tower with a shingled broach spire riding high on a wide brick west-end gable. Like so many Essex churches, St Giles's is kept locked, so you will be lucky to make your way inside and see the six timber posts and the braces holding up the free-standing belfry, the chancel's reredos of Moses and Aaron, and the great 13th-century parish chest cut from a single log.

Just beyond the church stands Mountnessing Hall, a beautiful building with a seven-bay facade of weather-darkened Georgian brick, tall chimneys and a pretty walled garden. St Giles's stands at its shoulder, the two buildings making a harmonious pairing like a long-married couple.

At St Giles's, follow the path (concrete 'FP' fingerpost) through the churchyard to the north-east corner, go through the hedge and bear left (649967) along the field-edge path with a hedge on your right. At the far end of the field, follow the field edge round to the left (blue and yellow arrows). In 130 yards (130m) turn right through the hedge (649971 – blue and yellow arrows), following a path in a woodland shelter strip. Leave the trees and keep ahead across a field to a road by a house (648975). Turn right for 200 yards (200m). Opposite Westlands Farm turn left; keep ahead to walk up the right side of Kitchen Wood, then continue ahead (651979) to reach the road at Tilehurst.

Westlands Farm (650975) and Tilehurst (652982) are two fine examples of their type. Westlands is a dignified, square Georgian brick house, with an ancient barn-cum-house beside it. The older building has a bulging, black-timbered end, and is topped by a weathervane fox. The fox has lost his brush – to some local sharpshooter, judging by the number of bullet holes in his body. Tilehurst is a great pile of a country house with many half-timbered gables in a vast acreage of brick under a lead-domed turret: a Gothic murder mansion behind its walls and railings.

Arriving opposite Tilehurst, bear left to reach the road. Turn right to reach Ingatestone Hall, from where you retrace your steps to the railway station.

11. ROCHFORD & PAGLESHAM

This fine long walk takes you way out into the wilds of easternmost Essex, a country divided between flat arable farmlands and muddy creeks. Wildfowl throng here, so the birdwatching is tremendous. You'll encounter stories of an 18th-century adventurer, and of a smuggler chief who munched wine glasses and wrestled a bull. Paglesham Churchend is one of Essex's most charming villages. Above all, the walk – the loneliest in this book – is steeped in the salty sights and sounds of the broad, tidal River Roach.

START AND FINISH: Rochford Station

LENGTH OF WALK: 14 miles (22km)

OS MAPS: 1:50,000 Landranger 178; 1:25,000 Explorer 176

TRAVEL: By rail from London Liverpool Street (50 mins); by road – M25 (Jct 29), A127 to northern out-skirts of Southend-on-Sea, B1013 to Rochford.

FEATURES: Rochford Hall; St Andrew's Church, Rochford; River Roach and its bird life (don't forget your binoculars and bird book!); Paglesham's two fine pubs; church and village street at Paglesham Churchend.

REFRESHMENTS: Plough and Sail PH, Paglesham Eastend; Punch Bowl PH, Paglesham Churchend; Cherry Tree PH on eastern outskirts of Rochford (890908).

From Rochford Station (873904) walk through the car park and turn left along the road. In 100 yards (100m) turn left along Hall Road ('Hockley, Rayleigh' sign). The road goes under the railway line, then bends right; keep ahead here along a tarmac lane, passing St Andrew's Church and, in the near distance, Rochford Hall (870903).

Rochford Hall and St Andrew's Church

'Rochford Hall,' says Rochford Hundred Historical Society's blue plaque by the front door of the house, 'Home of the Boleyn family, 1515 to 1542'. A strange attribution, since this fine Tudor house with its four gables and octagonal corner turret was probably built around 1545. Whatever the house that stood on the site then, it is claimed to be the birthplace of Anne Boleyn around 1504. Her father, Sir Thomas Boleyn, was created Viscount Rochford in 1525 by King Henry VIII, who was to involve himself closely, and disastrously, with this Essex family. Poor, doomed Anne, with her passionate red hair and her rumoured 'devil's teat' sixth finger, seemed destined for a strange fate. Failing to present her husband the king with a son and heir, she was beheaded at the Tower of London in 1536 by a French swordsman specially shipped over to London for the occasion.

The adjacent St Andrew's Church boasts a tall three-storey brick tower. The church walls are a characterful mishmash of clunch blocks, ragstone and flint, with crude chequered battlements of flushwork (knapped flint and freestone) to the south porch and south aisle. The north side of the church, with its two half-timbered gables and tall brick chimneys, looks remarkably like a medieval house.

Walk past the hall and church. Soon the lane enters a golf course. Keep ahead with a hedge on your left. Follow the hedge end round and make your way, following the footpath markers, over the golf fairway (take care! Flying balls!) to a white wicket gate and railway crossing (diagonally on your left, about 200 yards (200m) up the fence). Cross the railway (875900). This crossing is on the level – so please stop, look and listen! Keep ahead along the cul-de-sac to cross a road (877900 – concrete BW fingerpost and yellow arrow) and keep ahead along Tinkers Lane (don't take the private road). In 300 yards (300m) turn left, following a fenced path beside a car pound. At the end (879902) turn right along the Roach Valley Way (RVW) beside the River Roach. In ½ mile (0.75km), at Stambridge Mills, cross the river mudflats on a footbridge and follow the path round the buildings. At the road turn left (887904 – RVW symbol and yellow arrow); in 70 yards (70m) go right (RVW and concrete FP fingerpost) across a field and a reed pond by a footbridge.

The Roach Valley Way symbol is a Canada goose flying over a reed bed on a broad river, with a church tower peeping among trees in the background. It sums up perfectly the character of the River Roach landscape. The river itself, inland of its estuary, is a winding, muddy stream fringed with reeds and sedges and overhung with alder and poplar trees, a moody watercourse in tune with its flat, lowland landscape.

From the footbridge keep ahead through trees to cross a cricket field. At the road (891904) bear right along a green lane (RVW); at the bottom turn left along the River Roach, on a seawall path that runs for 5½ miles (9km) to Paglesham Eastend. The only deviation necessary is at Barton Hall (913913), where the seawall disappears. There's a fingerpost here that leads you on a track for ¼ mile (0.4km) around Barton Hall and its buildings to rejoin the seawall just beyond the farm.

An Ardent Adventurer

Where you join the river bank, spare a look back towards Stambridge Mills and the scatter of rusty trawlers among the yachts and dinghies in the marina. Between you and the mill stands the river-bank house of Broomhills (888903). In the late 18th century it was the home of John Harriott, a most remarkable adventurer. Born in the parish of Great Stambridge in 1745, this ardent youth catapulted himself into a rackety, exciting life after reading *Robinson Crusoe*. He started off by voyaging to New York as a midshipman in a Royal Navy warship. Soon he had embroiled himself in a romantic mystery involving rescuing an Irish woman from captivity and returning her to her family.

After cruising in the Mediterranean, Harriott had to be saved when his ship was wrecked. Nothing daunted, he volunteered for sea duty again, and was present at the attack on Havana, Cuba. After that he travelled east by sea to St Petersburg, then west again to Jamaica where he fought and survived a duel. By 1766 he was back in America, a sworn member of a Native American tribe. The settled life didn't hold Harriott, however: he was still no more than 21 years old, still full of pith and vinegar.

Off he went to India, to join the East India Company's campaign against Hyder Ali. During the fighting he was wounded, and shipped back home.

That put paid to the Essex Man's foreign jaunting. He took up the life of a farmer, along with dabbling in insurance broking. Harriott remained hot to handle, however. He lost all his money investing unwisely in the spirit trade. Sited as he was, here on the banks of a river notorious in that era for smuggling, he must have dabbled in the contraband 'free trade', too. But Harriott had his conscientious side as well (unless it was a clever blind), for he organised the first force of river police to patrol the Thames. All in all, a true 18th-century maverick.

Wildfowl Paradise of the Roach Muds and Marshes

Walking east along the seawall of the River Roach, two impressions strike home immediately: the extreme flatness of the landscape, and the tremendous abundance of birdlife. This eastern part of Essex lies very flat, and views across the fields run a long way. Willows, hedge oaks, pylons and the block-like shapes of houses and barns loom up against the sky as if magnified to twice the size. The rivers wind towards their North Sea mouths through fringes of salt marsh held together with thick tangled mats of sea purslane and seamed with sinuous tidal creeks. The Roach has built up

Opposite: Informal living quarters like these are a feature of the muddy, moody Essex coastal rivers.

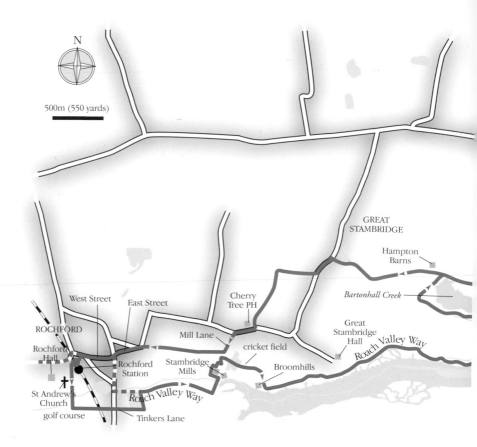

vast mudbanks, each square yard of mud packed with invertebrate and crustacean life. These flats make superb natural larders for waders, ducks and geese. In late autumn, millions of birds arrive from the Arctic Circle to spend the winter on the Essex estuaries, and the Roach gets its fair share. But these muds and marshes attract birds all the year round. Binoculars will enhance your enjoyment of the feeding, courting and squabbling of ringed plover, terns, redshank and curlew, with huge flocks of dunlin in autumn and skies full of

tumbling black-and-white lapwing; not to mention the omnipresent, ever-screeching gulls.

Murderer's Home Patch

The seawall path makes a big inland loop to encompass the marshy inlet of Bartonhall Creek. On the inner bank stands Barton Hall (913913), a modest enough farmhouse on a site that boasts a tremendous and tragic toehold in English history. In 1170 Barton Hall was the home of Sir Richard de Brito, a Norman knight keen to please his king. When Henry

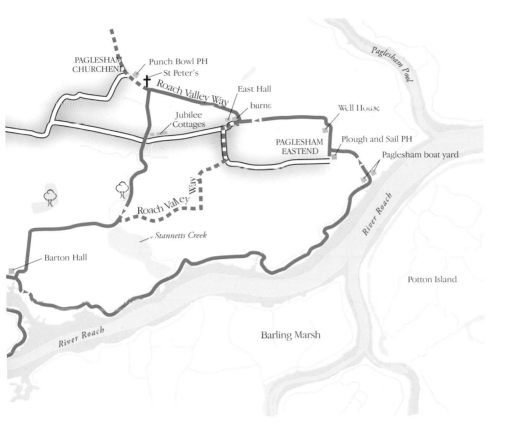

II delivered himself of his famous outburst, 'Is there none among the cowards that eat my bread who will rid me of this turbulent priest?', de Brito and his three infamous colleagues spurred for Canterbury, where they cut down the troublesome Archbishop, Thomas à Becket, in front of his own altar.

Paglesham Eastend

After the lonely, exhilarating miles, the return of civilisation is heralded by the big sheds and cranes of Paglesham boatyard and a rash of yachts at their moorings out in the river. The boatyard deals with every kind of repair from sizeable trawlers to the tiniest dinghies. When you reach the boatyard turn left down the steps and walk inland away from the seawall (note that there is also a FP sign here, a bit obscured by a big 'Private Road' sign). The clank of crane chains and chink of yacht halyards against masts accompany you as you turn inland through the boatyard (947921) and up the potholed lane through the widely scattered houses of Paglesham Eastend. Some are in candy-coloured brick, others are the traditional black-painted and weatherboarded Essex type. You reach a road, with the excellent Plough and Sail pub on your left (944923). This is a perfect Essex pub: small, weatherboarded, white-painted, with a red-tiled roof; inside it's low, beamy and friendly.

From the pub, return along the lane for 100 yards (100m); where it bends right towards the boat yard keep ahead (yellow arrow on gateway) past a garage, through a wicket gate and on up the left side of a field. Skirt Well House to reach a road (944927). Follow the road for ½ mile (0.75km) to East Hall (935927), where you turn right along the side of the first barn (concrete FP fingerpost and RVW) on the Roach Valley Way. Follow yellow arrows on to a farm track that doglegs round the back of East Hall. About 50 yards (50m) after it swings right, go left through a gateway (933928 – yellow arrow, RVW) and follow the field edge for ½ mile (0.75km) to St Peter's Church at Paglesham Churchend (926931).

Paglesham Churchend

St Peter's is a rugged old building, its stones eaten into uneven chunks by the winds and weather of flatland Essex. An avenue of pollarded limes leads to the door. The church boasts some nice medieval stone heads: a king, a nun and a queen, all gaping. The village of Paglesham Churchend consists of a single short street of houses: white-painted, weatherboarded, with flowers round their doors. At the western end of the street stands the three-storey Punch Bowl inn, white and weatherboarded like its neighbours. Inside are dark beams, low ceilings, winking horse brasses and a warren of nooks and snugs. Paglesham Churchend, in short, has charm to burn.

'Hard Apple', King of the Essex Smugglers

Charm was not one of the chief attributes of the famed and feared William Blyth, king of the area's notorious smugglers during the late 18th century. This clever and savage brigand, known as 'Hard Apple', was a real tough nut. He would munch broken wine glasses and drain a keg of brandy at a sitting, to impress and intimidate foes and friends alike. He once took on a bull in a wrestling match, and threw it to the ground.

Blyth's smuggling cutter *Big Jane* was well known to the excisemen. On one occasion they caught the Churchend gang red-handed, and ordered them to transfer their contraband kegs from *Big Jane* to the excise boat. While Hard Apple engaged the customs captain in a drinking bout below decks, his men found little resistance among the excise crew when they suggested broaching one of the brandy kegs. In no time the king's men were roaring merry, and the illegal kegs were being manhandled by the crafty smugglers back into *Big Jane's* hold.

Hard Apple was the churchwarden at St Peter's and found the church tower a very handy hiding place for contraband. The smuggler chief was a grocer by trade, and his customers would often find their purchases wrapped in pages torn from the church registers. Hard Apple died in 1830 aged 84, in the odour of sanctity. On his deathbed he had a chapter of the Bible and the Lord's Prayer read to him, and his last words as he turned his face to the wall were: 'Thank you. Now I'm ready for the launch.'

From the Punch Bowl return to the church, to where you have just come out of the behind-the-houses track. Turn right (FP fingerpost) along a field edge to the road at Jubilee Cottages (926925). Turn right along the road; then in 50 yards (50m) turn left through the hedge. Follow the path over the field to cross a stream by a metal footbridge. Follow the stream as it bends left, then, at its following right bend (926923), look ahead to see two clumps of trees. Two high-rise towers are visible in the distance. Aim for these towers across the field, passing the edge of a wood (924920) and keeping ahead to reach a bank that leads up to a large, lake-like body of water. On the lip of this turn right. In 100 yards (100m), at the corner, bear ahead (away from the water),

following RVW fingerposts along field edges for $3/4$ mile (1.25km) to Barton Hall (913913).

Rejoin the Roach Valley Way here and turn right along the seawall. In 300 yards (300m) the seawall swings away to the left (909913); descend from it and keep ahead here, following a field edge into a lane that leads through the farming settlement of Hampton Barns. Pretty Georgian cottages, stables and barns make a harmonious picture. Keep walking along this concrete track for $3/4$ mile (1.25km). At the road turn left and pass a lay-by on the right. In 100 yards (100m) turn right (897913 – concrete FP fingerpost) along a field edge with the hedge on your right. At the hedge end keep ahead (yellow arrow on post), and in 200 yards (200m) (893914) turn left (yellow arrow). Keep ahead along field edges to the road by the Cherry Tree pub (890908).

Turn right here along the pavement; in 150 yards (150m) turn left along Mill Lane. In 250 yards (250m) bear right (887905 – concrete FP fingerpost) on a field edge under two sets of pylon lines to reach a road (882906) on the eastern outskirts of Rochford. Keep ahead up the road to a T-junction. Turn left along the road, East Street, until it meets South Street (876905). Cross the road and walk along West Street to reach Rochford Station.

12. SHOREHAM, LULLINGSTONE & EYNSFORD

The River Darent's north–south valley is one of north Kent's most beautiful spots, and the walk from Shoreham to Eynsford and back does it full justice. Here are two castles to enjoy: one a poignant early Norman ruin, the other a handsome Elizabethan house. Shoreham and Eynsford villages boast some very attractive riverside scenes and a clutch of nice old cottages apiece. Shoreham has notable artistic connections with William Blake and Samuel Palmer. There's a remarkable Roman villa at Lullingstone, with the finest mosaic pavements unearthed in Kent. Above all, this expedition offers hours of walking through superbly lovely river valley scenery.

START AND FINISH: Shoreham Station

LENGTH OF WALK: 8 miles (13km)

OS MAPS: 1:50,000 Landranger 177; 1:25,000 Explorers 147, 162

TRAVEL: By rail from London Victoria; change at Bromley (50 mins); by road – M25 (Jct 4), A224 south for 1 mile (1.6km), minor road to Shoreham.

FEATURES: Shoreham village and church; river scenery in Darent Valley; Lullingstone Castle and St Botolph's Church; Lullingstone Roman Villa; Eynsford Castle; Eynsford old bridge and village.

REFRESHMENTS: Ye Olde George Inn, Shoreham; several pubs in Eynsford.

From Shoreham Station (526615) walk down the station approach, and at the A225 turn right down Station Road ('Shoreham Village' sign). Keep ahead for ¼ mile (0.4km) to reach Shoreham village and the Church of St Peter and St Paul (523616).

Church of St Peter and St Paul, Shoreham

This 14th- and 15th-century village church with its brick-paved yew avenue holds some notable treasures. You enter through an early Tudor south porch hewn from a single mighty oak. Inside on the west wall hangs a lively

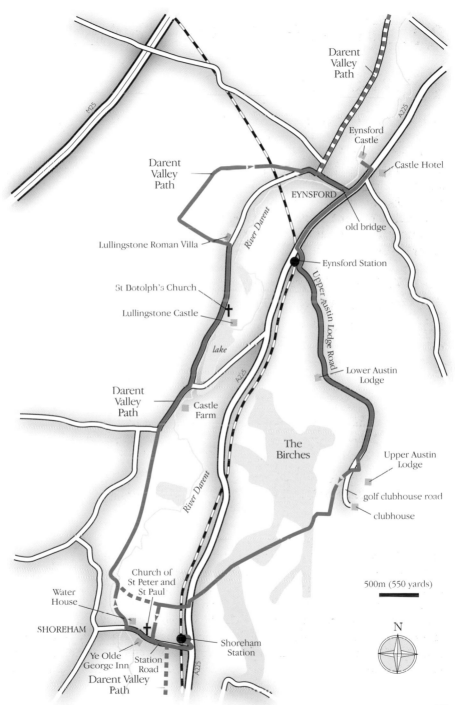

Darent
Valley
Path

Eynsford
Castle

Castle Hotel

Darent
Valley
Path

EYNSFORD

River Darent

old bridge

Lullingstone Roman Villa

Eynsford Station

St Botolph's Church

Upper Austin Lodge Road

Lullingstone Castle

lake

Lower Austin
Lodge

A225

Darent
Valley
Path

Castle
Farm

The
Birches

Upper Austin
Lodge

golf clubhouse road

River Darent

clubhouse

500m (550 yards)

Church of
St Peter and
St Paul

Water
House

N

SHOREHAM

Ye Olde
George Inn

Station
Road

Shoreham
Station

Darent Valley
Path

A225

painting by Charles Cope RA, showing Lt Verney Lovett Cameron of the Royal Navy, son of the Vicar of Shoreham, returning to the village church amid enthusiastic scenes after commanding the first European expedition to cross central Africa.

The church boasts a really fine 15th-century rood screen carved with a tangled trail of vine leaves and bunches of grapes. Its top bulges out, braced by finely carved vaulting; the Rood or great cross would have stood on top in pre-Reformation days. The organ casing, superbly carved, came from Westminster Abbey; some say that it encased the organ that Henry Purcell played there.

Water House

From the church continue along the village street, enjoying the handsome old brick houses with their high garden walls and neatly clipped hedges. Just before the bridge, bear right (521616 – 'Darent Valley Path/DVP' fingerpost) along the left side of Water House. This dignified, square, white-painted house behind its thick evergreen hedge often played host to William Blake (1757–1827), visionary poet and painter. One of the 19th century's best-known English watercolourists, Samuel Palmer (1805–84), stayed at Water House for several years as a member of a group of Blake's followers who styled themselves The Ancients. Palmer began his sojourns here in the year of Blake's death.

From Water House continue along the right bank of the River Darent. In ¼ mile (0.4km), DVP yellow arrows point left across a footbridge (520621), skirting round a mill house and on along the left bank of the river. Soon the path gently bends away from the river. Follow it (DVP yellow arrows and stiles) through the fields of the beautiful Darent Valley for 1 mile (1.6km).

The path runs past a hop garden with its giant cat's-cradle of wooden poles and wires. At the road (523634 – DVP fingerpost) bear right and keep ahead past Castle Farm and the Hop Shop, where you can buy hop bines, dried flowers and local produce of all sorts. Continue along the road (take care – it can be busy and there's no pavement!). In 300 yards (300m), where the road swings right, keep ahead (526638 – DVP fingerpost) through a kissing gate and back on to the riverside path (DVP). Follow it along the river for ⅓ mile (0.5km) past a rushing pool, to a road (529644). Lullingstone Castle is just ahead on the right.

Lullingstone Castle and St Botolph's Church

Lullingstone Castle is a handsome Tudor country house set on a lake

Opposite above: Lullingstone Castle has been in the possession of the Hart-Dyer family since Tudor times. Opposite below: The broach spire of St Martin's Church beckons you on over Eynsford's humpy bridge.

created by damming the River Darent. The approach is through the arch of a 15th-century brick gatehouse, which perfectly frames the house. The Peche family held the estate from 1361; since Tudor times it has been in the possession of the Hart family, styled Hart-Dyke since the Harts and the Dykes joined in marriage in the mid-18th century. A tour of the castle puts you in touch with intimate family history: portraits of the Harts with their long, intelligent faces and broad cheekbones persisting across 500 years; a poignant likeness of a tiny Hart boy (he died in childhood), still in skirts, clutching a bunch of cherries; the helmet worn by Tudor jousting champion Sir John Hart at the Field of the Cloth of Gold in 1520. There is also the grandeur attaching to an ancient and influential family: the magnificent Elizabethan plasterwork in the barrel-vaulted ceiling of the first-floor state drawing room, the great staircase inserted to flatter Queen Anne on her visit here and the elaborately carved bed provided for her.

To one side of the house stands St Botolph's Church. It's well worth glancing round the interior. The Flemish rood screen of 1500–20 is heavily carved with Tudor roses, foliage and peach stones ('pêche'), and the windows are filled with stained glass that ranges from willowy 14th-century saints in green robes to Tudor yellow-and-white roundels that include Jesus crucified on a vine shoot. There's a beautiful plaster ceiling, and the tomb of Sir George and Lady Elizabeth Hart guarded by cherubs with a spade and a skull, an angel with a laurel wreath, and a ghoulish shrouded skeleton. Also here is Sir Percyvall Hart, one of Queen Anne's principal courtiers (hence the queen's visit to Lullingstone). It is said that Sir Percyvall's daughter, Ann, jilted her fiancé, Sir Thomas Dyke, during their engagement party, sliding from her chamber window down a knotted-sheet rope to elope with and marry her lover, a naval officer named Bluet. After Bluet's death nine years later, however, Ann found the faithful Sir Thomas still willing, and they were finally joined in marriage.

From the castle continue along the tarmac track for ½ mile (0.75km), to where the outbuildings of Lullingstone Roman villa come into view. Just before you reach the first building, the path turns left up some steps in the woods (530650; fingerpost). Either proceed ahead to visit the villa, or follow the arrow up the steps to continue the walk.

Lullingstone Roman Villa

The protective building that covers Lullingstone Roman villa could qualify for the title of 'Kent's Ugliest', but the villa itself – unearthed on the west bank of the River Darent in 1939 – is Kent's finest. This splendid dwelling, built first in timber around AD 75, but later solidly rebuilt in flint cobbles and tiles, was preserved for posterity by the lucky accident of its location, at the foot of a steep slope. Over the centuries, soil washed down the hill, and covered the villa with an earthy, protective blanket.

Nearly 30 rooms are clustered together in a nest of flint-walled spaces. They include cellars, a bath-house, bedrooms, a kitchen, verandas and living rooms. On the walls of a 4th-century chapel the excavators found fragments of decorated plaster which, when pieced expertly together, revealed figures of Christians praying with outstretched arms. Also decorating the walls was a Christian 'Chi-Ro' or Christ monogram. Older faiths were also practised at Lullingstone: witness the niche painting in the well cellar, depicting a water goddess with water flowing from her nipples and reeds sprouting from her hair.

Of all the artefacts on display, the chief treasure is the wonderful mosaic pavement laid in the floor of the dining room-cum-audience chamber. The lower panel shows a graceful, naked Europa being abducted by a rampant Jupiter in bull-shape (a winged cupid grabs the bull by the tail in a vain attempt to slow things up). The upper panel depicts a red-cloaked Bellerophon astride Pegasus (the winged horse), his right hand stabbing a long lance through the back of a not-very-threatening chimera. This panel also contains some jolly, bulgy sea beasts, and has at its corners three of the four seasons (summer is missing). A riot of geometrical symbols fills the space between the two panels, including swastikas, triangles, hearts and shaded crosses. The contrast between the formality of the geometrical designs and the free-flowing expressionism of the classical panels is breathtaking. This is certainly one of the finest pieces of Roman art discovered in Britain.

From the villa, return along the track until you are just beyond the first of the outbuildings, and bear right up steps (DVP arrow and 'Lullingstone Park Circular Walk' fingerpost). Climb the path up the field edge for 500 yards (500m). At the top of the field turn right (525652 – DVP yellow arrow on a post) and follow the path with a hedge on your right. Where the hedge ends keep ahead across the field on an obvious footpath. In 1/3 mile (0.5km) cross a tarmac track and continue down a field to cross the railway – please take care (533657). Continue down across the next field to reach the road in Eynsford. Keep forward round a right bend. In 20 yards (20m) the DVP turns left, but keep ahead here (537657 – 'Eynsford' sign) to cross a bridge (or the ford!) and reach the A225. Turn left along the village street. Opposite the Castle Hotel, turn left ('Village Hall' sign) down an alley to find Eynsford Castle (542658).

Eynsford Castle

Eynsford is a charming village, full of nice old brick and weatherboarded houses, many with photogenic clusters of tall chimneys and oversailing upper storeys. The castle was one of the first built in stone by the Normans, a great many-sided stronghold that was never strengthened by the addition of battlements. The castle builders evidently expected things to be peaceful among the subdued tribes of the Darent Valley. The flint walls stand 30 feet (9m) tall; there are archways, doors and windows, and the remnants of a 12th-century dwelling within the rugged, gloomy grey ruins.

From the castle return to the A225 and turn right to walk the length of the village (pavements all the way). Just before the road goes under the railway bridge (536650), bear left past Eynsford Station and continue along Upper Austin Lodge Road for 1½ miles (2.5km) to reach Upper Austin Lodge. The Austin Valley is a beautiful side cleft off the Darent Valley, its chalky fields swooping and rolling like immense, smooth sea billows. There is an old wooden oast and a working forge at Lower Austin Lodge, and a valley road that peters out ²⁄₃ mile (1km) further up at Upper Austin Lodge. Apart from the rattle of trains on the nearby railway line there are few outside sounds to disturb the peace of this delectable 'lost valley.'

The road passes through the gates of Upper Austin Lodge (542637). Soon the road divides; take the left fork ('Private Road, No Entry' sign). In 100 yards (100m) bear right over a stile (542631 – yellow arrow and 'Footpath to Shoreham' sign). Cross the golf course clubhouse road and continue along the valley bottom with a hedge on your left. At the end of the second field turn right between hedges (539627) and climb the valley slope to turn left inside the bottom edge of a wood. In 150 yards (150m) the track bears right and climbs steps to leave the wood just short of the crest of the ridge (537625). Keep forward here on a grass track, steering a little to the right to enter Preston Hill Plantation (534624; fingerpost signs).

The path forks immediately; take the left-hand path. In ⅓ mile (0.5km), at another fork (530622), a yellow arrow on a post points right. This path soon dips steeply downhill, past a flagpole and on down. At the foot of the slope leave the trees and cross a house drive. 'Footpath' signs direct you on along another woodland footpath, then across a field to meet the A225 (527619). Cross the road (with great care!) and turn left along it for 60 yards (60m), then right (FP fingerpost and DVP post) to cross the railway by stiles (please take care). Keep forward down the field with the hedge on your left. At the end of the hedge turn left (524619 – yellow arrow) along the field bottom to the road in Shoreham (523615). Turn left to reach Shoreham Station.

13. TEYNHAM, CONYER & THE SWALE

Moody, muddy and magnificent – that sums up the character of this fine walk through the north Kent apple orchards and along the banks of the broad Swale, the tidal channel that separates the Kentish mainland from the Isle of Sheppey. Beautiful at any time of year, maximum enjoyment comes in spring (apple blossom time) or autumn (fruit harvest); though winter is wonderful along the Swale too, if you are well wrapped up, thanks to the multitudes of overwintering wildfowl that throng the channel. There are two fine churches to enjoy en route (you'll need to plan ahead to get St Mary's, Teynham unlocked – see page 196), and one of the best pubs in Kent, the darkly atmospheric Ship Inn at Conyer.

START AND FINISH:	Teynham Station
LENGTH OF WALK:	10½ miles (17 km)
OS MAPS:	1:50,000 Landranger 178; 1:25,000 Explorer 149
TRAVEL:	By rail from London Victoria (1 hr 20 mins); by road – M25 (Jct 2), M2 (Jct 5), A249 to Sittingbourne, A2 to Teynham.
FEATURES:	Orchard landscape; Ship Inn, Conyer; bird-watching along the Swale (don't forget your binoculars!); St Mary's Church, Luddenham; St Mary's Church, Teynham.
REFRESHMENTS:	Ship Inn, Conyer; Three Mariners PH and Castle Inn, Oare.

From the platform at Teynham Station (957631) bear left over the bridge, descending to a lane that leads into open fields. You're faced with a choice of three paths; take the track that leads in front of a row of cottages, continuing along a green footpath. In 100 yards (100m) it turns right (956632) and runs between a sewage works and allotments. Soon a hedge comes in on your right; keep it there for ½ mile (0.75km) as you walk north-north-east through orchards.

Fruit and Malaria

The silt and clay of these north Kent soils, combined with the mildness of the climate, make this excellent country for fruit growing. Although many of the orchards have been grubbed out in recent years and replaced by grassland or arable fields, much of the flat country hereabouts is still given over to stumpy apple, pear and cherry trees. When the pink or greeny-white flush of spring blossom is on these acres of geometrically drilled fruit trees, the effect is stunning.

Cherries were first cultivated in the region by Richard Harrys, one of the Tudor era's most green-fingered and forward-looking experts. Harrys was fruiterer to His (extremely demanding) Majesty King Henry VIII, so it was important to get things right if head retention was on the agenda. The royal fruiterer planted 105 acres (about 40ha) with cherry trees imported from Flanders, and the area never looked back. Teynham became southern England's centre of fruit growing in Tudor times, famous for 'the sweet Cherry, the temperate Pipyn'. The trade continued to flourish through the centuries, and the most senior locals can still remember the red-sailed cherry barges that would carry the fruit to Covent Garden and other London markets.

But things were not always so smooth and prosperous around Teynham. Only just north of the village stretched the freshwater marshes, reclaimed from the sea, where stagnant puddles of water were perfect breeding grounds for malarial mosquitoes. 'He that will not live long, Let him dwell at Murston, Teynham or Tonge', warned the local doggerel. Medieval Teynham was notorious for its exaggerated rate of death from 'marsh ague' or malaria. Part of the problem was the work of the monks in building seawalls along the Kentish shoreline, enabling malarial marshes to develop at the same time as they were strengthening the area's sea defences and increasing its value for agriculture. The Roman shoreline had run just inland of the present-day one, and the Romans tended vineyards on terraced slopes here. But by the late Middle Ages the populace had been forced to move inland to healthier areas.

In $\frac{1}{2}$ mile (0.75km) cross a footbridge (961642) and follow the left bank of a reedy ditch beneath power lines and on to the road in Conyer (963645) where there's a fingerpost cluster with sets of markers for the Saxon Shore Way (SSW) and Swale Heritage Trail (SHT). Go straight ahead here along the road (SHT), to reach the Ship Inn at the end of the road (961648).

Conyer and the Ship Inn

In Victorian times Conyer was a little brick-making port, sending bricks out by the barges that would load up at the wharf in the mouth of Conyer Creek. Conyer was one of a thousand maritime or estuarine villages around

Opposite: Don't fret if you are too late for blossom time around the Teynham orchards; come in early autumn to see the ripe apples at their finest.

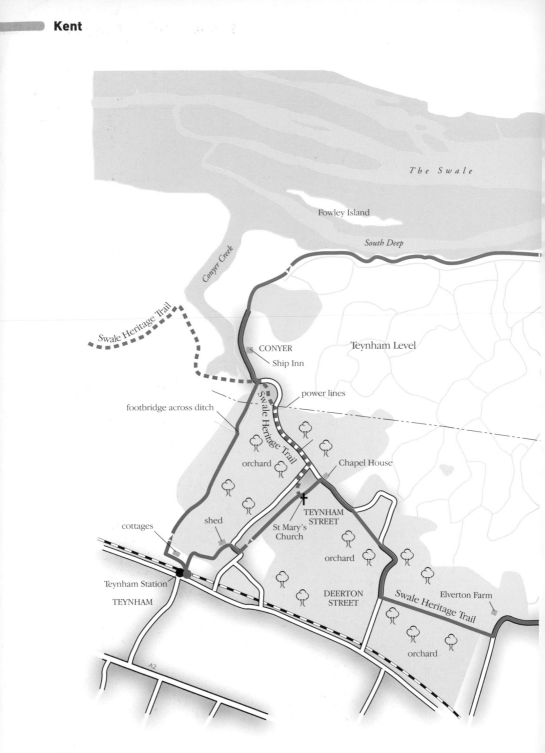

The Swale

Fowley Island

South Deep

Conyer Creek

Swale Heritage Trail

CONYER

Ship Inn

Teynham Level

power lines

Swale Heritage Trail

footbridge across ditch

orchard

Chapel House

TEYNHAM
STREET

cottages

shed

St Mary's
Church

orchard

Teynham Station

TEYNHAM

DEERTON
STREET

Swale Heritage Trail

Elverton Farm

orchard

A2

orchard

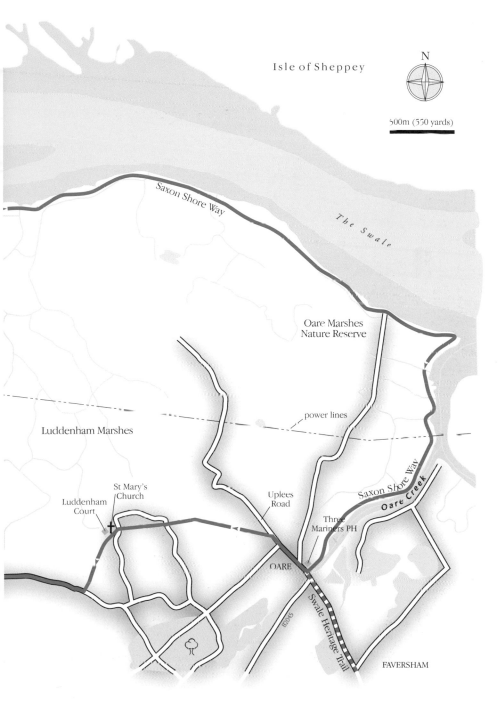

Isle of Sheppey

N

500m (550 yards)

Saxon Shore Way

The Swale

Oare Marshes
Nature Reserve

power lines

Luddenham Marshes

Saxon Shore Way

Oare Creek

St Mary's
Church

Luddenham
Court

Uplees
Road

Three
Mariners PH

OARE

Swale Heritage Trail

B2045

FAVERSHAM

the coasts of Britain that maintained a lifeblood of coastal commerce from their little wharves, jetties or quays. Railways, and then road transport, along with the gradual silting-up of these muddy outlets, put an end to a hugely diverse, small-scale commercial trade. Conyer's Ship Inn is a throwback to those more leisurely days – an end-of-the-road inn out on a limb; dark, firelit and friendly; a pub with books in its bar and great local conversation round its tables – you'll find it hard to tear yourself away.

From the Ship Inn walk forward; go through a turnstile and on along a concrete path (SSW). Keep ahead on a path leading across rough ground, partially paved with old Conyer bricks, to the seawall path along the Swale (966655). Direction finding is easy for the next 5 miles (8km): just follow the path east to the mouth of Oare Creek (018646), then turn right and walk inland along the creek to Oare village.

Birdwatching Along the Swale

The Swale is the swirling, tidal channel that separates the Isle of Sheppey from the shore of north Kent. Rather more than a mile wide here, the Swale was a formidable obstacle before the first Kingsferry Bridge was built in the 1860s. Ferry boats were the only way of getting on and off the island, and during this section of the walk you pass the sites of two of them: Elmley Ferry where you join the seawall path, and Harty Ferry at the far end of the Swale. The Sheppey shore seems low and dark as you look across the water. Nearer at hand you pass Fowley Island ('island of fowl'), where you may spot owls or harriers. The creeks and mudflats of the Swale provide a wonderfully rich larder for wildfowl; regulars include curlews, redshanks, oystercatchers, turnstones, grebes and lapwings, with big crowds of brent geese, dunlins and wigeons in season. You might see plovers, shelducks and teals, ragged grey herons and sleek deadly sparrowhawks. Binoculars are a walker's best friend here. It's no wonder that the Swale has been declared a site of international importance for overwintering wildfowl.

Explosion on the Marshes

In the 19th century Oare Marshes were reclaimed largely for the purpose of building a big explosives factory. The manufacture of guncotton began here around 1870, quickly followed by other explosives including nitroglycerine, cordite and TNT. The chickens came home to roost, however, in the middle of the First World War. On 2 April 1916, 165 tons of TNT and ammunition blew up with a concussion that was felt nearly 100 miles (160km) away in Norwich. One hundred and sixteen workers died in this, the worst munitions explosion in UK history. Production of explosives stopped after the First World War. In the 1960s local conservationists defeated a plan to turn the marshes into a marina, and they are now administered as a nature reserve – exactly the destiny one would have hoped to see them fulfil.

From the seawall path turn right along Oare's main street to pass the Three Mariners pub. In 250 yards (250m) keep ahead down Uplees Road for 30 yards (30m), then turn left over a stile (004630 – SHT marker), and walk diagonally across the fields to cross a lane (997631). From here, aim straight between the oast towers and the church tower at Luddenham Court, to reach St Mary's Church (992631).

Luddenham Court and St Mary's Church

When medieval Luddenham Court was built, the area was probably still tidal, with the sea washing twice daily up against the low ridge on which the farmstead stands. Together with the big oasts for drying hops, the barns and the outbuildings, house and church form a tranquil, nucleated ensemble that can hardly have changed over the passing centuries.

Luddenham Court is private property, but the owners run a farm shop. The red-brick tower of St Mary's was put up in 1866 to replace one that tumbled down, but the main body of the little church is essentially Norman, with some thin Roman tiles reused to fortify the walls. It's a plain interior, stripped of its pews, entered through a low round-headed doorway. On the nave floor by the font lies a cracked Purbeck marble coffin lid of the 14th century, carved in high relief with a cross and two hands raising a chalice – or perhaps it's a crown.

To continue the walk, retrace your steps and face the oasts where you'll see a fingerpost pointing left and right. Bear right and follow markers across the fields to a road (991626). Turn right along the road for ³/₄ mile (1.25km). At the entrance to Elverton Farm (981628), follow the road round a left bend. In 150 yards (150m) turn right (SHT sign) for ¹/₂ mile (0.75km) on a path along the edges of orchards. A ¹/₄ mile (0.4km) along the path, cross over a concrete road, keeping a tall evergreen hedge to your left. At Deerton Street turn right along a road (972629), which soon bends left. Just beyond the following right bend, go left through a gap (972633 – SHT sign) and keep a hedge on your left to reach a road. Keep forward through Teynham Street. Opposite Chapel House turn left over a stile (968638 – FP fingerpost and SHT sign) to Teynham's St Mary's Church.

St Mary's Church, Teynham

The large cruciform church – 12th century in origin, though what one sees today is largely 13th-century work – seems curiously imposing for its isolated position among a handful of scattered farms. This 'Cathedral of the Orchards' was built to reflect the glory of the archbishops of Canterbury, who had a palace just to the west of the church. Many archbishops spent a good deal of their year here in medieval times.

The exterior of the church under its 15th-century tower looks rugged and weather-beaten. The rough walls contain slivers of Roman tiles. You enter through a fine 15th-century oak door that contains several deep bullet holes; the shots were fired by Roundheads who were besieging a party of Royalists barricaded in the church after a nearby Civil War skirmish. Inside the church a short length of wide-link chain is fixed low down in the south wall; local legend says that Oliver Cromwell attached his horse to it while stabling the beast in the church.

In spite of its size, St Mary's has a homely feel, perhaps because of the criss-cross of rafter-like beams in the roof and the two lattice-panel clerestory windows, high in the south wall, that would better suit a domestic setting. Under the choir floor carpet you'll find a brass to William and Elizabeth Palmer (1639), both in handsome Stuart dress. The north transept carpet conceals a small-scale brass to William Wreke (1533) in a merchant's robe, and another to Robert Heyward (1620), and to two children – one a long-haired boy, the other a baby tightly wrapped in swaddling clothes. Under the south transept carpet is a splendid brass to a fully armoured John Frogenhall, his feet resting on a faithful dog.

Leave St Mary's by the lychgate and walk along the lane. In 25 yards (25m), where the lane bends right, keep ahead (965636) on a fenced path through orchards and rough ground to meet a road (961633). Turn right for 100 yards (100m), then left into a farmyard to bear left along the front of a big corrugated shed. Walk along a driveway ('pedestrian' sign). In 150 yards (150m) turn right along a fence (959632). In 100 yards (100m) the path turns left between fences to reach Teynham Station.

14. HOLLINGBOURNE, THE NORTH DOWNS WAY & THURNHAM

Four miles (6km) of exhilarating downland tramping along the North Downs Way (NDW) form the backbone of this walk, and the views from the crest of the downs are truly stunning. Hollingbourne is a charming village, its street lined with handsome old houses. The Elizabethan mansion of Hollingbourne Manor was home for centuries to the Colepepers, an eminent Kent family, and All Saints Church contains many memorials to them. It's worth seeking out the unique and beautiful Colepeper Cloth, a genuine labour of love. At Thurnham you can pay your respects at the grave of the Mighty Mynn, one of the titans of 19th-century Kent cricket.

START AND FINISH:	Hollingbourne Station
LENGTH OF WALK:	8 miles (13km)
OS MAPS:	1:50,000 Landranger 188; 1:25,000 Explorer 148
TRAVEL:	By rail from London Victoria (1 hr 15 mins); by road – M25 (Jct 3 or 5 (to join M26)), M20 (Jct 8), A20 towards Lenham for ½ mile (0.75km), left to Hollingbourne.
FEATURES:	Old houses in Hollingbourne; Colepeper Cloth; Colepeper and Gethin monuments in All Saints' Church, Hollingbourne; views south from North Downs Way; Mighty Mynn memorial at the Church of St Mary the Virgin, Thurnham.
REFRESHMENTS:	The Dirty Habit PH, Hollingbourne; Black Horse Inn PH, Thurnham.

From Hollingbourne Station (834551) walk down the long station approach. Turn left under the railway; in 150 yards (150m) turn left (840549 – FP fingerpost) along a footpath to All Saints' Church in Hollingbourne (843551).

Hollingbourne's Famous Trencherman

There are several very fine medieval houses in Hollingbourne, a village which seems to have been passed over by the outside world. But it attracted a tabloid-style fame in the early 17th century because of the eating habits of one of its residents, Nicholas Wood. He was a famous trencherman, who once entered a wager to eat at one sitting as much black pudding as would stretch across the River Thames between London and Richmond. Wood's obsession with eating went far beyond such stunts, though. Contemporary reports say that he would 'devour at one meal what was provided for twenty men, eat a whole hog at a sitting, and at another time thirty dozen of pigeons'. The poor man was obviously suffering from a rampaging eating disorder. Medical men of the time named it 'caninus appetitus', Hound's Hunger. Wood died a pauper in 1630, having spent all he possessed on food.

All Saints' Church, Hollingbourne

In All Saints' Church you'll find several monuments to the Colepeper family of Hollingbourne Manor. The most striking is in the north chapel, dedicated to the family, with 124 stone heraldic shields on the walls (only two still retain their painted devices) and the centrally placed white marble effigy of Lady Elizabeth Colepeper who died in 1638 aged 56, 'the best of women, the best of wives, the best of mothers'. Her feet rest on a freakish-looking animal, snub-nosed and snarling, with a dog's head, leopard's spots, a cow's tail and cloven hooves: a 'thoye', one of medieval heraldry's more curious beasts. On the north chancel wall is a memorial to Sir John Colepeper, a brave Royalist who fought at the battles of Naseby and Keinton, and went into exile with the king-in-waiting, Charles II.

The Colepeper Cloth

While Sir John was in exile his four daughters embroidered what is known as the Colepeper Cloth – perhaps as an altar cloth, or maybe as a pall for a coffin. It took the young women 12 years and cost one of them her eyesight, ruined through so many hours of close work by candlelight. The cloth is not on public show, but can be viewed by prior arrangement. It is a beautiful work, a 6-foot (2-m) long rectangle of purple velvet surrounded by a broad border of Kentish fruits worked in coloured dyes and gold thread: acorns, cobnuts, pears and plums, pomegranates with star-like flowers, mulberries and quinces, peaches and grapes. All these were embroidered on to coarse linen, then stitched to the work with gold thread. A border of angels separates the inner

Opposite: Classic Kentish views on a walk around Hollingbourne and Thurnham – timbered houses under steeply sloping red tiles, and out in the country the fence-maker's art on display.

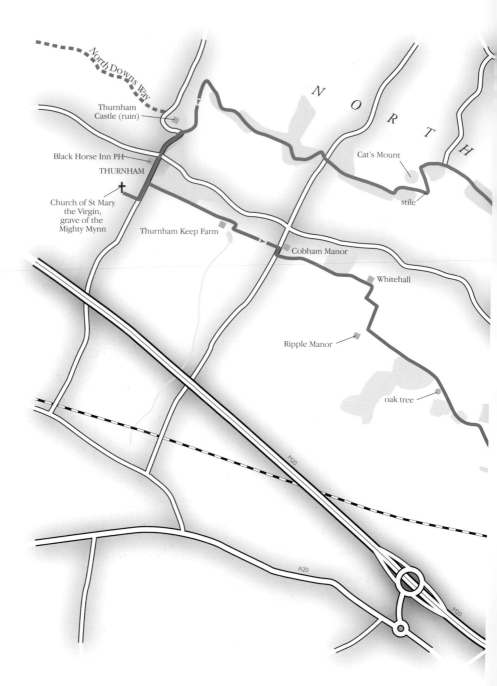

North Downs Way

Thurnham
Castle (ruin)

Black Horse Inn PH

THURNHAM

Church of St Mary
the Virgin,
grave of the
Mighty Mynn

Thurnham Keep Farm

Cat's Mount

stile

Cobham Manor

Whitehall

Ripple Manor

oak tree

N O R T H

M20

A20

M20

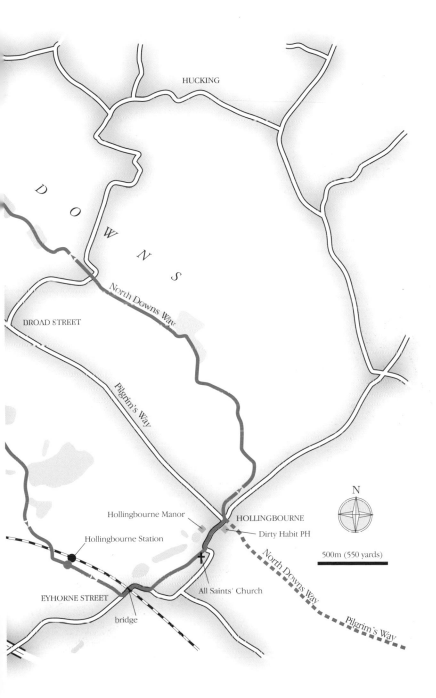

HUCKING

D O W N S

North Downs Way

BROAD STREET

Pilgrim's Way

N

Hollingbourne Manor

Hollingbourne Station

HOLLINGBOURNE

Dirty Habit PH

500m (550 yards)

North Downs Way

Pilgrim's Way

EYHORNE STREET

bridge

All Saints' Church

rectangle of velvet from the frame of fruit, and another angel border follows the outer edge of the piece. It is a remarkable and moving work of art, and a testament to daughterly devotion.

From the church, walk through the lychgate and turn left up the road, passing the big brick-built Tudor house of Hollingbourne Manor and continuing up the village street. Pass over the crossroads above the Dirty Habit pub, and in 50 yards (50m) bear left (845554 – North Downs Way/NDW fingerpost) up steps and along a path among trees, then along a field edge to go through a kissing gate. A NDW yellow arrow and acorn symbol points out the path, climbing open ground diagonally left to a post seen above. Turn left here (847557 – yellow arrow) along a track for 200 yards (200m); pass through a kissing gate and continue, gaining height on a snaking track to the top of the downs.

Ancient Trackways of the North Downs

The North Downs Way National Trail shadows the course of the Pilgrim's Way, the medieval pilgrim path from Winchester to the shrine of St Thomas à Becket at Canterbury. The pilgrims themselves were treading in the footsteps of travellers who had beaten out the ancient trackway over 5,000 years: drovers, then merchants, warriors and others. The old road kept just below the crest of the downs on their southward side, a course that afforded shelter from the weather, a grandstand lookout, and concealment from the eyes of potential enemies. From the North Downs Way you enjoy a largely uninterrupted southward panorama over 30 or 40 miles (50–70km) of rolling, beautiful Wealden country, thickly wooded, with the blue line of the South Downs closing the far horizon.

These long scrubby grassland slopes make a wonderful chalky habitat for lime-loving plants: wild thyme, cowslips, salad burnet, marjoram, and a number of beautiful orchids. Chalkhill blue butterflies flitter over the slopes, which are grazed by sheep; grazing and scrub control are vital pieces in the jigsaw of management of this Area of Outstanding Natural Beauty.

The North Downs Way continues north-west along the crest of the downs. Walk straight for 3/4 mile (1km), keeping ahead under power lines (843565), to reach a T-junction of tracks (842566) at a Hucking Estate notice. Turn left here for 100 yards (100m), then right (NDW yellow arrow) and on through trees for 1/2 mile (0.75km). At OS grid reference 836581 you cross a lane (FP fingerpost). Keep ahead along the fenced path to enter a field through a kissing gate. Keep ahead here, crossing the field to enter trees (NDW arrow). Follow NDW markers through scrubby trees for 1/2 mile (0.75km) to join a muddy bridleway. Follow it downhill out of the trees as it swings south around Cat's Mount. Watch out for the NDW arrow on a post on the left of the track; turn right over a stile here (825577), climb to cross another stile and keep on up between a yew grove and a fence. Continue for ½ mile (0.75km), descending steps to cross a lane (818578 – NDW fingerpost). Keep ahead along the North Downs Way, ignoring the FP fingerpost on the left in 50 yards (50m).

In ⅓ mile (0.5km), the North Downs Way turns off to the left (816580 – NDW arrow), descending and then ascending steps. Continue for ⅓ mile (0.5km) to leave the trees over a stile (812582). Keep a fence on your left, climbing a slope to turn left and descend into the head of a dry valley. Go left over a stile here (NDW arrow) and follow the path down the right side of the valley. At a road (868580) leave the North Downs Way and turn left downhill into Thurnham. Pass the Black Horse Inn pub (806579), and in 300 yards (300m) turn right along a path (805576 – 'St Mary's Church' fingerpost) to the Church of St Mary the Virgin.

The Mighty Mynn

On the north side of St Mary's, the Mighty Mynn rests under a yew tree. Alfred Mynn (1807–61), the 'Lion of Kent', was a genuine 19th-century cricket hero, a 17-stone (108-kg) round-arm fast bowler and ferocious batsman. He was born at Goudhurst, but lived for many years in Thurnham. With the ball the Mighty Mynn could 'maintain a terrific pace for hours without fatigue'. With the bat he was a whirlwind. In 1836 he

made four consecutive scores of 283 – two of these not out.

The Lion of Kent was a man with open hands and a big heart, according to his memorial stone: 'His kindness of heart and generosity of disposition during many years of public life as the Champion of English cricketers endeared him to a large circle of admiring friends. His widespread popularity is attested by the circumstance that four hundred persons have united to erect this tombstone, and to found in honour of a name so celebrated the Mynn Memorial Benevolent Institution for Kentish Cricketers.'

From the church return up the road. In 150 yards (150m) turn right (805577 – PB21, at Thurnham Keep Cottage) along a lane to Thurnham Keep Farm. Pass the twin oasts or hop-drying kilns, and keep ahead along a field-edge path with a hedge on your left, to cross a stile into a road (815572) at Cobham Manor. Turn right for 50 yards (50m); just past a weatherboarded oast house, turn left (FP fingerpost in the hedge) through a gate and across the oast-house courtyard (it looks private, but the public footpath runs this way), aiming for the yellow arrows on the gate ahead of you; then through three gates in quick succession, aiming ahead all the while. Pass through a gate, then up steps in a bank and over a stile (816572 – yellow arrow). Keep ahead along a fenced path through a horse paddock; cross a stile, and then aim a little left to leave the field over another stile. Go through a gate in a belt of trees (yellow arrow). Continue with the hedge on your left to cross another stile (820570 – yellow arrow). Keep ahead across scrubby ground for 20 yards (20m) to cross another stile and walk along a fenced path to Whitehall, where you go through two wicket gates to a road (821570 – BW fingerpost).

Turn right along the road. It doglegs left, then right. In another 150 yards (150m) turn left at a 'Ripple Manor' sign (821567 – yellow arrow on post) along a field edge and up the left side of a wood. At the wood end (826563 – yellow arrow) aim diagonally right for a lone oak tree, then continue to the left corner of the wood beyond (827561 – yellow arrow on post).

Field Path Back to Hollingbourne

This field path back to Hollingbourne through the low valley landscape makes an enjoyable contrast to the previous high-level striding along the North Downs Way. All around are vast hedgeless fields, farms like little settlements with their cottages and converted oasts, and blocks of woodland that break up the broad arable vistas.

From the wood's corner, aim for the right corner of a short strip of trees, and from here bear left to the bottom right corner of the wood ahead (829560 – yellow arrow on post). From here, aim ahead for 300 yards (300m) to where the field is divided by a line of trees. Here you are faced with a huge field. Turn right, and skirt the field edge, passing by a wood and along the foot of a railway embankment, until you reach a plank bridge in the bottom left corner of the field. Cross the bridge (832552 – yellow arrow) and continue along the field edge. In 100 yards (100m) turn right across the railway through kissing gates – please take care. On the far side turn left along the hedge; in 150 yards (150m) bear left over a stile and along a path to Hollingbourne Station.

15. NEWINGTON, LOWER HALSTOW & THE MEDWAY ESTUARY

Three very fine old churches form the punctuation points of this walk through the apple orchards and along the seawall of a lonely peninsula that sticks up from the north Kent coast into the wide tidal basin of the Medway Estuary. You may find any or all of these churches locked, but keyholder details are posted at each church (contact the church keyholders several days in advance in order to avoid disappointment, see page 197). The peninsula is one of those remote characterful outposts that you are constantly surprised to discover so close to London. Make the most of this walk in spring when the fruit trees are in full blossom.

START AND FINISH:	Newington Station
LENGTH OF WALK:	7 miles (12km)
OS MAPS:	1:50,000 Landranger 178; 1:25,000 Explorer 148
TRAVEL:	By rail from London Victoria (1 hr approx.); by road – M25 (Jct 2), M2 (Jct 5), A249 towards Sittingbourne, A2 towards London for 1½ miles (2.5km). Park near Newington Station.
FEATURES:	Orchards, salt marshes and mud creeks; Medway Estuary and view to Isle of Grain; Church of St Mary the Virgin, Newington; St Margaret of Antioch church, Lower Halstow; St Mary's Church, Upchurch.
REFRESHMENTS:	Three Tuns, Lower Halstow; Crown Inn, Upchurch.

From Newington Station forecourt (859650) walk down Station Road. In 20 yards (20m), turn left along an alleyway opposite No. 41, and left along Church Lane under the railway line and on to a crossroads (861653). To see the Church of St Mary the Virgin, turn right here past Church Farm House with its oasts and half-timbered rear portion to reach the church (862653).

Church of St Mary the Virgin, Newington: Judgement Day

The weather-beaten tower of St Mary's, striped in bands of flint and ragstone, dominates the nearby countryside. This is a remarkable church, well worth the effort of arranging entrance with the keyholder (see page 197). Among many treasures it contains a lovely spidery 700-year-old purlin roof over the south chancel; a brass in the chancel floor showing Alice, wife of Sir John Norton and of John Cobham, Esq., in full Elizabethan dress; a huge iron-banded trunk chest; and some humorously carved demons on a 15th-century priest's desk. But the church's chief glory is its wonderful display of wall-paintings dating from around AD 1340 on the north and north-east walls. These include an epic Doomsday with the righteous rising from sheltering coffins at the blast of trumpets blown by angels, while the damned bare their teeth in the agonies inflicted by a horrifically masked Devil. There is also a Nativity with a shawled Virgin and a figure of St Joseph stroking his brow, overcome with awe; and saints painted on the window splays, one of them a bald and luxuriantly bearded St Paul with a sensual mouth and large, expressive eyes. Don't miss this treat of a church.

At the church gate lies one of those large stones called sarsens ('saracens', or 'foreigners', because of their uniqueness in a neighbourhood), this one known as the Devil's Stone. Legend says that the Evil One, disturbed by the church bells, climbed the tower and put them in his sack. But when he leaped down from the tower with the bells on his back he landed awkwardly on the stone, tripped over and rolled down the hill into a stream.

Back at the crossroads, turn right ('Lower Halstow') down Wardwell Lane (NB this is a narrow stretch – watch out for cars!). In 200 yards (200m), turn left on a right bend (861655; FP fingerpost) through a damp, rushy valley where watercress beds once flourished, crossing footbridges and stiles. You emerge from scrub bushes at the foot of a slope (860660); bear left up the slope, aiming to the left of a pylon, to cross the left-hand of two stiles. Follow a path under power

Opposite clockwise: St Mary's Church at Newington with neighbouring oasts; someone's pride and joy moored up at Halstow Quay; 'Cherry pink and apple blossom time ...'.

lines and on over the broad back of Broom Downs to reach a road on the outskirts of Lower Halstow (859669). Turn left, then immediately right along a path with a stream on your left. In 300 yards (300m) turn left across a footbridge and down an alley, turning right at the end to a T-junction (859672). The Three Tuns pub is just along to the right, and beyond it you'll see St Margaret of Antioch church (865674).

St Margaret of Antioch Church, Lower Halstow

The walls of St Margaret of Antioch are a crazy mixture of stones, flints and Roman tiles – there was a brick and tile works at Lower Halstow during the Roman occupation some 1,700 years ago. The stumpy church tower has a pointed cap, and the north angle of the tiled roof slopes almost to the ground. Armed with the church key (see page 197) you can admire the nave with its late Saxon or early Norman herringbone tiles, and the remnants of medieval wall paintings – these include, on one of the south nave arches, a manticore, a fabulous monster with a lion's body, a man's head, porcupine quills and a scorpion's sting.

There's also a beautiful Norman font with relief carvings of angels and kings – which has a nice story attached to it. The First World War saw anti-aircraft batteries sited around Lower Halstow, and the concussion of their heavy explosions often caused damage and breakages in the village houses. After a particularly nasty night the parson's wife entered the church and was appalled to see pieces of the font scattered on the floor. Yet the font itself appeared undamaged. A quick examination unlocked the mystery. What everyone had always taken to be a stone font was in fact a lead one, heavily plastered over at some point in the past – conjecture said, by Royalists during the Civil War to prevent Roundhead soldiers melting the font down for bullets. It was the plaster covering that had fragmented and fallen to the floor under the shock waves of the explosions.

At the crossroads by the Three Tuns pub, cross the road and walk past the 'Private – No Parking' sign (there's a concrete FP marker in the grass verge). Pass 'Moorings' to reach Halstow Wharf.

Halstow Wharf and the Medway Estuary

Saxon monks named Halstow 'Halig Stow', the 'holy meeting place'. A busy brick works (closed in 1966) used to stand beyond Halstow Wharf, conveniently placed to send its products away via the Medway Estuary whose tides lap the northern edge of the village. These days all that is left of the brick works is a number of raggedy brick heaps buried in weeds.

From Halstow Wharf you continue along the Saxon Shore Way long-distance path, skirting the salt

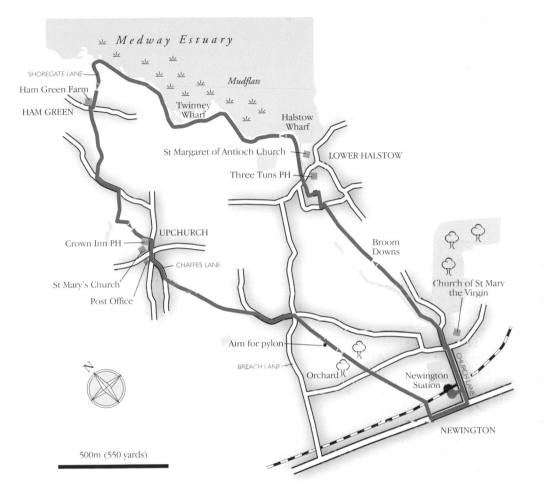

marshes of Halstow and Twinney Creeks and following Saxon Shore Way arrows/SShW.

North of Halstow Wharf opens the big green-blue bay of the Medway Estuary. On its seaward horizon, occasionally nodding and dipping, stand the navy-blue and white giraffe shapes of the dockside cranes on the Isle of Grain where the Medway meets the River Thames. The Saxon Shore Way runs along the seawall, looking over a vast expanse of mudflats with islets of salt marshes, scruffy grass and green spikes of glasswort. Curlews and oystercatchers send their plaintive whistles and cries up from the mudbanks around Twinney Wharf, where old Thames barges and coasters lie at relaxed angles in the creeks, adapted in more or less seamanlike fashion for the water-gypsy lifestyle. Inland, the apple orchards stretch away to lonely farmhouses.

After 1½ miles (2.5km) you reach Shoregate Lane (850691), where you turn inland (SShW) along the road for ¼ mile (0.4km) to Ham Green Farm (847688). Turn right along the road, and in 20 yards (20m) turn left (SShW FP in the hedge). Follow a track through orchards and past riding stables (SShW) to reach a road (844683). Turn left (SShW); in 250 yards (250m) turn right (SShW FP) across a field. At the far side (843679) go through a kissing gate with a fishing lake on your right. The Saxon Shore Way bears right round a bend here, but you turn left ('public footpath' arrow) along a hedge and then across paddocks into a housing estate. Turn left to a T-junction, then right up The Street, past the Crown Inn pub to find St Mary's Church on your right (844675).

St Mary's Church, Upchurch

St Mary's spire resembles one candle-snuffer on top of another. Inside the church, the south wall has a 14th-century chalk arcade with lions and a Green Man spewing flowers from his mouth. The south chancel features lovely medieval glass showing an angel playing a hurdy-gurdy; the north aisle has some superb blue glass. The list of vicars includes Edmund Drake (vicar from 1560–67), father of Sir Francis Drake. On the south wall is a 13th-century fresco of St Spiridon of Cyprus pouring gold pieces from his chasuble. The saint turned a snake into gold to help a poor farmer, and reconverted the gold into snake when the farmer repaid the loan.

Opposite Upchurch post office turn left down Chaffes Lane. In 200 yards (200m) turn left opposite Bradshaws Close (844672), taking the right-hand of two footpaths (stile and FP fingerpost), across a succession of paddocks through kissing gates for ⅓ mile (0.5km). At the far side turn right over a stile (846667), then bear left around the edge of a paddock. On the far side turn left over a stile (847666, yellow arrow) down a path to a road (848665). Turn right to reach a crossroads with Breach Lane (851663). Go through a kissing gate and aim directly for a pylon; then keep the same line over fields and on through an orchard to its top right corner (853658). Turn left over a stile, across a field and between paddocks to cross a road (854655). Continue the same line across a large field to go under the railway line (856650). Keep ahead to the A2; turn left to Station Road and left again to Newington Station.

16. BOROUGH GREEN, IGHTHAM MOTE & OLDBURY HILL FORT

This walk explores one of the most delightful countrysides in Britain – the steep fields, apple orchards and deep-sunk valleys of the northern Kentish Weald. Here are woods of oak, sweet chestnut and hazel, carpeted with bluebells in spring; and other woods of silver birch and pine that have grown to cover old commons with plenty of heather and bilberry still in evidence. Two very special sites claim attention along the way: the huge Iron Age hill fort of Oldbury, one of the largest such strongholds in the south of England; and the National Trust's medieval moated manor house of Ightham Mote, beautiful in half-timbering and stonework, with enough ghosts and tangled old stories to satisfy everyone in the family.

START AND FINISH:	Borough Green and Wrotham Station
LENGTH OF WALK:	8½ miles (13.5km)
OS MAPS:	1:50,000 Landranger 188; 1:25,000 Explorer 147
TRAVEL:	By rail from London Victoria (45 mins); by road – M25 (Jct 5), M26 (Jct 2a), A20 to Wrotham Heath, A25 to Borough Green.
FEATURES:	Pretty houses and millpond at Basted; woods and apple orchards between Basted and Yopps Green; oasts at Yopps Green; Ightham Mote moated medieval house; old heathland under trees on Respit Hill; Oldbury Iron Age hill fort.
REFRESHMENTS:	Mote Restaurant, Ightham Mote; George and Dragon, Ightham.

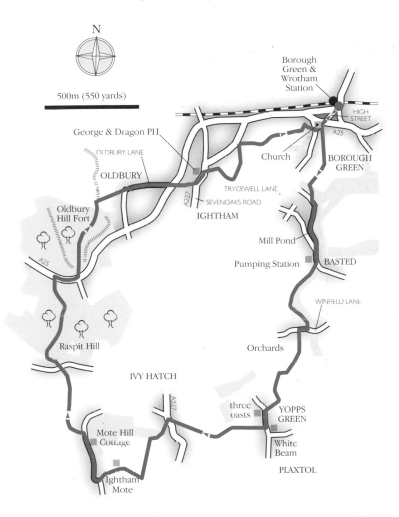

N

500m (550 yards)

Borough Green & Wrotham Station

HIGH STREET

George & Dragon PH

OLDBURY LANE

OLDBURY

Church

A25

BOROUGH GREEN

A227

TRYCEWELL LANE

SEVENOAKS ROAD

Oldbury Hill Fort

IGHTHAM

Mill Pond

A25

Pumping Station

BASTED

WINFIELD LANE

Raspit Hill

Orchards

IVY HATCH

A227

three oasts

YOPPS GREEN

Mote Hill Cottage

White Beam

PLAXTOL

Ightham Mote

From Borough Green and Wrotham Station (609574), turn right over the railway. On the following right bend, keep ahead along Borough Green's High Street (with National Westminster bank on your right). Cross the A25 at the end, and continue along Quarry Hill Road ('Church'). Opposite the church, turn left (608572, FP fingerpost) and follow the footpath south out of Borough Green, crossing a couple of roads and keeping the same direction, to descend through woods to a road near Basted millpond (607563). Turn left past the pond.

The Beautiful Basted Valley

This is a gorgeous spot, sunk deep in its valley of trees: the disused millpond with its ducks and coots; the old mill house (the mill buildings are long

121

gone); a broad picnic lawn; and then a line of immaculately designed modern houses interspersed with some handsome old cottages with the characteristic Kentish upper storey weatherproofed in mellow red tiles. This is quintessential Kent, the garden of England: huge old garden cherry trees frothing with pink blossom in spring; neatly kept vegetable gardens and mown lawns; an air of absolute peace and quiet in the narrow valley; all set against high wooded banks on both sides of the stream.

You pass a Southern Water pumping station on your right, and at the foot of Plough Hill fork right (607557) through the woods along the valley bottom. At Winfield Lane (606550) turn right uphill for 100 yards (100m); then turn left over a stile (fingerpost) and on through an orchard. Cross a river and continue up a stony lane between orchards for ²/₃ mile (1km) to the road in Yopps Green (602542).

Woods and Orchards

The Basted Valley woods, rather overgrown and neglected, form a rich tangle of creepers, fallen willows, boggy pools and pungent patches of wild garlic. The full-grown oaks and sycamores are the haunt of chiffchaffs, blackcaps, wrens and other songbirds in spring and summer. Sunk among the lush dampness you'll spot the squared shapes of former watercress beds, their spillways and channels still pouring water through the overgrown and redundant system. Soon you find yourself climbing a stony lane between apple orchards with far views across the folds of the Kentish Weald, to emerge by the three conical oasts (or hop-drying kilns) at Yopps Green.

At Yopps Green turn left along the road past the three oasts. Opposite White Beam house turn right (602540; concrete bridleway marker) along a bridleway. Keep heading west over crossing paths for ¹/₃ mile (0.5km) to a T-junction of paths at the top of a rise (596539). Turn right ('bridleway') for ¹/₃ mile (0.5km) through woods to the A227. Cross the road (591541); bear left through a gate and along a bridleway (fingerpost). In 200 yards (200m) bear half-right over a crossing of paths (591539) and continue along the wooded ridge. Follow the path downhill beside a hedge; at the bottom, turn right along a lane (589534) to reach the road at Ightham Mote (584534).

Ightham Mote, a Gem of a Moated House

This is one of the National Trust's treasures; a gorgeous Tudor house that envelops within its stone, brick and timber frame a 14th-century Great Hall and solar, the whole complex

Opposite above: Ightham Mote, the Tudor house with the Gunpowder Plot ghost.
Opposite below: Oasts at Yopps Green, once fragrant with drying hops, now form features on a village house.

crowned by towering chimneys and acres of tiles, rimmed by a moat and set to scenic perfection in its wooded valley.

Walking round the house, you are struck by the small scale of everything, and by the pokiness and darkness in which our forebears lived their lives. Some of the rooms – the Great Hall of 1320, the solar, the neat bedrooms with their priceless 18th-century Chinese wallpaper as fragile as tissue – have grandeur and a largeness of effect, but the sombre linenfold panelling and the heavy dark timbers give a poignant impression of shadowed domesticity, like a Dutch Master's interior.

'A vile and papisticall house' as it was styled in a Catholic-bashing report of 1585, Ightham Mote is said to contain a priest's hole, built for sheltering Roman Catholic clergymen in those turbulent times when a priest, if discovered, could expect to be hanged, drawn and quartered – an unspeakable death. The house nevertheless has an equivocal place in Catholic mythology, for a persistent story says that it was Dame Dorothy Selby of Ightham Mote who unwittingly betrayed the Gunpowder Plot of 1605 by writing a letter to her cousin Lord Monteagle warning him not to be among those who attended the opening of Parliament. 'They shall receive a terrible blow this parliament', said the note, 'and yet they shall not see who hurts them.' In fact the writer wasn't Dorothy Selby, but Monteagle's brother-in-law Francis Tresham. Yet the legend has Dorothy dragged to a hole

in the wall in Ightham Mote, fastened up there and left to starve to death. Her skeleton was said to have been found by workmen repairing the wall in 1872. There's no evidence for any of this – but no one has told the ghost of the Grey Lady who continues to haunt the house.

To continue the walk, keep on between the house (on your right) and the lake (on your left). Bear left at the end, then through gates and right up the road for ⅓ mile (0.5km), passing Mote Hill Cottage on your right (583538). In 100 yards (100m) bear left ('bridleway') up a woodland track for ½ mile (0.75km) to cross a road (580546). Climb steeply uphill ('bridleway'). At the top the path doglegs left and right to reach a crossing bridleway (579547). Turn left for 50 yards (50m), then right (blue arrow) down steps and on northwards across the wooded land of Raspit Hill for a good ½ mile (0.75km). Pass ponds to reach the A25 (579555). Turn right for 200 yards (200m), cross the road with great care to the central reservation, then on to a bus stop at the far side. Fork right here past a National Trust 'Oldbury Hill' notice, on a bridleway that rises through the trees.

Oldbury Iron Age Hill Fort

You are following an ancient trackway that originally ran from the south Kent coast to the North Downs. In 200 yards (200m) you can detour to the left or right to walk a circuit of Oldbury's ramparts. These man-made earth banks, now smothered in tall oaks and sweet chestnut coppice, enclose the 124 acres (50ha) of one of Britain's biggest Iron Age hill forts. Hut circles, grain pits and many artefacts have been excavated here. The active life of the hilltop stronghold was short, a century at most. Oldbury was constructed some time between 100 and 50 BC by a native Wealden tribe, captured from them by the warlike Belgae, and then overrun by the Romans as they advanced up the old track towards the River Thames at the start of their invasion in AD 43.

The bridleway soon levels out. Follow it north for ¼ mile (0.4km) to a five-way junction of tracks (582560). Bear half-right ('bridleway') and follow this bridleway, crossing various paths, for another ¼ mile (0.4km) to a T-junction at the northern edge of the

trees (584564). Turn right down a bridleway here to follow Oldbury Lane to the A25 (592565). Cross and go down Sevenoaks Road opposite. At the A227 turn left, then right up Trycewell Lane opposite the George and Dragon pub (595566). In 150 yards (150m) bear right up a path just before an oast (fingerpost). In 200 yards (200m), at the top of a bank (598566), bear left along a fence. Just before the A227, turn right along a path (599570), under power lines and across a minor road (602570). Continue along the path for ¼ mile (0.4km). At a housing estate turn left, then right up Tilton Road. By a 'Staley Avenue' sign, keep ahead up a short path. Turn right at the end, then left up Quarry Hill Road (607571) to return to the station.

17. HEVER & CHIDDINGSTONE

Two castles dominate this walk through the woods and clay farmlands of the Kentish Weald: Hever Castle, where the ill-fated Anne Boleyn spent her childhood and where she was later wooed by King Henry VIII; and Chiddingstone Castle, a Tudor house comprehensively turreted and castellated in fine romantic Gothic style in the early 19th century. Chiddingstone village is a tiny Tudor and Jacobean gem, with its ancient (and maybe druidical) Chiding Stone tucked away in the trees behind the main street. Woodland paths connect these varied delights, leading you through some of west Kent's loveliest countryside.

START:	Hever Station
FINISH:	Cowden Station
LENGTH OF WALK:	7 miles (11km)
OS MAPS:	1:50,000 Landranger 188; 1:25,000 Explorer 147
TRAVEL:	By rail from London Victoria (55 mins); by road – M25 (Jct 5 or 6), A25 to Westerham, B2026 to Edenbridge, minor road to Hever.
FEATURES:	Hever Castle; St Peter's Church, Hever; oast houses and oak woods of the Kentish Weald; Chiddingstone Castle; St Mary's Church, village houses and Chiding Stone at Chiddingstone.
REFRESHMENTS:	King Henry VIII Inn PH, Hever; Hever Castle restaurant and tea room; Castle Inn, Chiddingstone; Rock Inn, Hoath Corner.

Opposite above: Everyone's dream of a snug Kentish village is caught in this view of Chiddingstone in springtime.
Opposite below: The Chiding Stone where, according to local lore, scolds were brought to be taught to hold their tongues.

From Hever Station (465445) walk down the station approach to turn right along the road. In 50 yards (50m) turn left ('Public Footpath to Hever') along a fenced path. In 300 yards (300m) go through a kissing gate. Keep ahead across the field to pass through two kissing gates, then across another field. A kissing gate leads into a green lane (471447), where you turn left to a road. Turn right, and in 50 yards (50m) left (brown 'Hever Castle' sign). The road rounds a right bend; just after this, turn left over a stile (474448 – FP fingerpost and concrete footpath marker). In 100 yards (100m) turn right through a gate (yellow arrow) and across the corner of a field to cross a stile. Keep the hedge on your left for 100 yards (100m), then cross through it (arrows, marked path) and walk up the right side of the hedge to cross a stile into the road. Turn right for 100 yards (100m) to find the gatehouse of Hever Castle on your left (476449).

Henry VIII and Anne Boleyn at Hever Castle

Hever Castle is one of England's most romantic castles – partly for its moat-girt position, cradled in a beautiful wooded valley, but chiefly because of the extraordinary and poignant love story that was played out within its walls. The tale of the love affair, marriage and deadly quarrel between King Henry VIII and Anne Boleyn is a famous one that never fails in its romantic appeal. It was here that ill-starred Anne spent much of her early childhood, and here that Henry came as an ardent lover to court and win the beautiful 'Greensleeves' as his queen. The ghost of poor witchy Anne still haunts the castle.

Hever Castle was begun in 1270 as a fortified gatehouse and walled bailey inside a moat. In the late 15th century Sir Geoffry Bullen, a Norfolk man made good, bought the castle. It was his grandson Sir Thomas Bullen (or Boleyn), Anne's father, who built a Tudor house within the walls; its half-timbered walls and mellow brickwork survive there. Anne was born around 1501, perhaps at Hever, and was just 12 when her ambitious father sent her to attend Queen Margaret of Austria at Brussels. Soon afterwards, Anne went to learn her manners and gain a sheen of sophistication at the French court, where she stayed until she was about 21. When she came back to England, groomed and polished, it was not long before King Henry's eye fell on her. Henry was married to Catherine of Aragon, but Catherine had failed to provide him with a male heir. He desperately wanted to divorce her and try for an heir with Anne Boleyn, but the Pope refused to countenance such a thing. The most extraordinary convulsions in English political and religious life ensued. Henry, in his passion for Anne and his furious disappointment with Catherine, would have his way, no matter what. So he initiated a permanent split with the Church of Rome, swept away the monasteries, and set up a new church

with himself at its head. He married his Kentish love in January 1533; she was already pregnant with the future Queen Elizabeth 1.

The portraits of Anne that hang at Hever Castle present her as attractive, elliptical of glance, potentially beguiling, but not of a beauty as devastating as one might expect, given her effect on the king. But all her charms and wiles availed Anne nothing when she failed to produce the male heir Henry needed. Three years after their marriage he was looking round again, with his eye on Jane Seymour. Anne was clapped into the Tower of London on trumped-up charges of adultery and incest, and on 19 May 1536 she was beheaded on Tower Green by a French swordsman specially commissioned by His Majesty.

Tour of the Castle

A tour of the castle unfolds the story of Henry and Anne, the star-crossed lovers, and also tells the saga of the building's restoration in the early 20th century by William Waldorf Astor, the American multi-millionaire. Meticulous care was taken; for example, local craftsmen recreating 'Tudor' plaster ceilings were ordered to use the authentic materials that would have been employed by Tudor plaster workers, and to do their work 'by eye' alone, using no straight-edge measurement tools. Heavy Edwardian woodcarving lends weight and dignity to the various rooms, and a superb collection of 16th-century portraits of the key players in the 'Henry and Anne' drama brings history vividly to life. Perhaps the most poignant item on display in the castle is the 15th-century Book of Hours, gloriously handwritten and painted in Bruges around 1450, which belonged to Anne Boleyn. On the opening page of the penitential psalms appears, in Anne's faded handwriting, the inscription 'Le Temps Viendra, je Anne Boleyn' – 'My Time Will Come'.

Outside are beautiful gardens, formed from boggy meadows at the behest of William Waldorf Astor. They include a formal Italian garden, a fine geometric hedged maze, a curious bushy 'water maze' and a walk along the shore of the 35-acre (14-ha) lake that took Astor's workmen four years to dig and fill.

In St Peter's Church, just outside the castle gate, you will find the tomb and brass of Sir Thomas Bullen, Anne's father. Follow the path through the graveyard, taking the left-hand fork, and continue through trees. This soon becomes a fenced path, shadowed by a private lane. Between the trees to your left there are glimpses of fine parkland and a gleam from the big lake. The path runs through the woods; then, $3/4$ mile (1.25km) after leaving Hever, it passes by a house (488448). Follow Eden Valley Walk/EVW waymarks past Bothy Cottage and on along a fenced path that crosses a road (491447 – FP fingerpost). Keep ahead along a muddy fenced path, along wood edges, and over scrubland of coppiced chestnut (there are several EVW waymarks). Descend through a little rock cutting and continue forward between cottages. At the road, turn left (498447) to reach the gate of Chiddingstone Castle (497453) on your right in $1/2$ mile (0.75km).

Chiddingstone Castle

It was the Streatfeild family, local ironmasters grown rich through Wealden iron production, who built the core mansion of Chiddingstone around 1500. Three hundred years later Henry Streatfeild provided the house with crenellations, octagonal towers and turrets to turn it into a proper Gothic-style castle. The early

20th century saw a steep slide in the castle's fortunes, the nadir being reached after years of neglect and abuse while it was requisitioned during the Second World War. Then, in 1955, the art connoisseur and romantic Denys Bower bought Chiddingstone Castle and filled it with his eclectic collections of pictures, Buddhist temple art, Jacobite relics, Japanese porcelain and lacquer and Egyptian antiquities. The tour of the house shows off these extremely diverse treasures, collected by a man who was careless of his own comfort – he lived in the most ramshackle conditions in the castle, whose fabric he could not afford to repair – but who had an unerring eye for excellence.

Chiddingstone Village

From the castle gate walk forward to the crossroads. Turn right ('Chiddingstone' sign) to walk through Chiddingstone village. Chiddingstone, now in the care of the National Trust, is a wholly charming short strip of 16th- and 17th-century houses. The exterior walls of the Castle Inn are hung with dusky red earthenware tiles, its windows are diamond-panelled, its floors tiled.

Along the street, the 15th-century Burghesh Court used to be Chiddingstone's manor house. Anne Boleyn's father bought it in 1517. Now it houses a shop and tea room. Opposite the shop stands St Mary's Church, whose parishioners have worked the church kneelers with local themes: the castle, oast houses, the rectory, Kentish flora and fauna, and Zippy the church cat.

The Chiding Stone

From the church continue along the village street to pass the school. Turn right here through a gate ('footpath to Chiding Stone' fingerpost) to follow a path to the Chiding Stone (501451). This handsome sandstone outcrop (not the first one you come to – the real stone is 10 yards (10m) beyond) is shaped like a cottage loaf and stands some 13 feet (4m) high. It is an obvious, natural gathering place, and has been suggested as a site for druidical ceremonies, and maybe sacrifices. Nagging village wives were said to have been brought here to be admonished publicly: hence its title of the Chiding Stone. But Chiddingstone probably got its name more mundanely, from the 'ing' (or settlement) of a Saxon farmer named Cedd.

From the Chiding Stone return to the road and turn right. In 20 yards (20m) go right along a fenced path; pass the village playing field, pass a stile and continue. Keep following the path across an open field, to walk down the left side of a copse for 20 yards (20m). Turn right over a stile (yellow arrow). On the other side the path forks; take the right fork through the trees, and in 20 yards (20m) pass a pond on your right. Keep ahead towards the barns of Hill Hoath Farm, to cross a stile (EVW waymark) where the road divides. Bear right down a gravelled track to reach a road opposite 'Withers' house. Bear left here down a private road between cottages to pass a gate (EVW and blue arrows). In 30 yards (30m) bear left (yellow arrow) to cross a stile (497446, yellow arrow). Keep a fence on your left and follow yellow arrows on posts to cross a stile in the top right corner of the field (495442). Turn left along a fenced path (yellow arrow) into woods. In 100 yards (100m) join a muddy, rutted track. In 100 yards (100m) keep your eyes peeled for a fingerpost on the left of the track; turn left here (493438 – yellow arrow on post) through trees, then on across open grassy ground to reach a yellow arrow on a post. In 100 yards (100m) bear left through trees (492434) to cross Trugger's Gill. Emerge, and keep a fence on your left across two fields, where it becomes a fenced path leading to a road (495431). Turn left for 150 yards (150m) if you want to visit the Rock Inn at Hoath Corner (a country pub classic!); otherwise turn right along the road for ¹/₂ mile (0.75km) to a T-junction (490428).

Go over the T-junction, through a gate (FP fingerpost) and along a lane. In 300 yards (300m) a footpath fingerpost points right; cross the field here to a kissing gate in the far bottom corner, to continue in the top edge of Bilton's Gill wood. Fifty yards (50m) before the edge of the wood trends left (486422), the path forks. Take the right fork steeply down through the trees to cross a footbridge and climb to cross a stile and leave the trees. Keep the hedge on your left for 200 yards (200m), then keep a cattle trough on your left and head for the skyline. Once there, you will see a house near the far left corner of the field. Pass beside the house, keeping the hedge on your right, into another field; keep ahead to reach a track by way of a gate in the far right corner of the field (482418). Turn left along the track for 150 yards (150m); at a T-junction turn right for 400 yards (400m) to a road (478418). Bear left here, downhill, and in 200 yards (200m) turn right ('Cowden Station' sign) to Cowden Station (476417).

18. DORMANSLAND, HAXTED MILL & LINGFIELD

This walk passes by green lanes and stony tracks through a particularly beautiful tract of east Surrey. You'll see Lingfield's racecourse, the moated site of Starborough Castle, Haxted Mill with its restored wooden milling machinery, and one of Surrey's best collections of medieval tomb monuments in Lingfield parish church. There's a bonus, too – there are no fewer than three places where you can stand with one foot in the eastern and one in the western hemisphere! Note: there is one very short (150 yards (150m)), nasty stretch of road in this walk. If you wish to avoid it (which means missing out on visiting Haxted Mill), follow the alternative route as described in italics.

START:	Dormans Station
FINISH:	Lingfield Station
LENGTH OF WALK:	9 miles (14km)
OS MAPS:	1:50,000 Landranger 187, 1:25,000 Explorers 146, 147
TRAVEL:	By rail from London Victoria or London Bridge (50 min approx.); by road – M25 (Jct 6), A22 south to Blindley Heath, B2029 to Lingfield, minor road to Dormans Station.
FEATURES:	Lanes and woodlands of east Surrey; Starborough Castle moated site; Haxted Mill; Church of St Peter and St Paul, Lingfield.
REFRESHMENTS:	Plough Inn, Dormansland; Riverside Brasserie, Haxted Mill; Star Inn, Lingfield.

From the platform at Dorman's Station (396415) climb the steps and turn left along the front of the station building, then immediately left (FP fingerpost) along a tarmac path over a common. In 300 yards (300m) the path reaches a crossroads (398416), where you turn left along unmarked Mill Lane.

Mill Lane and the Meridian
The crossroads on Mill Lane lies exactly on the Greenwich Meridian – oo of

133

longitude – so those with a leg stretch as wide as their imagination can bestraddle the seam of the world! Mill Lane is rough-surfaced, leaf-carpeted and sun-dappled. Through gaps in the hedge you soon get views over the white-railed gallops of Lingfield Park racecourse, which has been hosting race meetings for well over 100 years.

Soon you cross the railway (397418), then a golf course begins to your left. Continue along Mill Lane into woods. In 200 yards (200m) turn right at a crossroads of tracks (396424 – '18th Tee' fingerpost). In 150 yards (150m), blue arrows on a post on the right of the track point you to the right on a gravel path that crosses the golf course (beware flying balls!) and runs beneath the railway (399426). At West Street keep ahead along a residential lane to cross a road (403427 – FP fingerpost). Continue along the path to another road, where you turn right for 200 yards (200m) to a crossroads (406428 – Plough Inn to the right). Cross over and keep ahead along Ford Manor Road. In 300 yards (300m) pass Ford House and take the right fork in the road ('Greathed Manor' sign and PB fingerpost).

Pass the entrances to Greathed Manor and Ford Manor (416425), keep ahead ('Courtyard' sign) and follow fingerposts with horseshoe logos. In 200 yards (200m) the path splits beside a pond. Take the left fork up the left side of a weatherboarded barn (418424);

follow the track sharply to the left here, then round a right bend in front of buildings in red-and-black brick. The track continues into trees, then as a hedged path through the fields to pass Littleworth Cottage (424426). In 50 yards (50m) follow the lane as it bends left; in another 50 yards (50m) where the lane bends right, bear left through a gate along a green lane. Skirt a small wood, and keep ahead on the far side (horseshoe fingerpost) to a road (423434). Bear right for 20 yards (20m), cross the road, then cross a stile (Vanguard Way/VW yellow arrow and FP fingerpost). Walk diagonally across the field, aiming about two-thirds of the way up the opposite hedge to cross a stile (425437), and turn left along the driveway to Starborough Castle (426441).

Starborough Castle

Through the railings you catch a glimpse of trees, landscaped banks and flowerbeds, statues and water features – also of a Georgian battlemented summer house and a fine, dignified, brick house. But Starborough Castle itself, built by the 1st Lord Cobham in the 1340s, has long vanished from its square moated site.

The Cobhams were one of the greatest families of medieval England, friends and confidants of many kings and queens. The 3rd Lord Cobham fought at the Battle of Agincourt in 1415 and, as a mark of respect, was granted

Opposite above: Flat fields and slow, snaking watercourses are characteristic features of the landscape between Starborough Castle and Haxted Mill. Opposite below: Dwelly Farm sits perfectly framed among the east Surrey fields and woods.

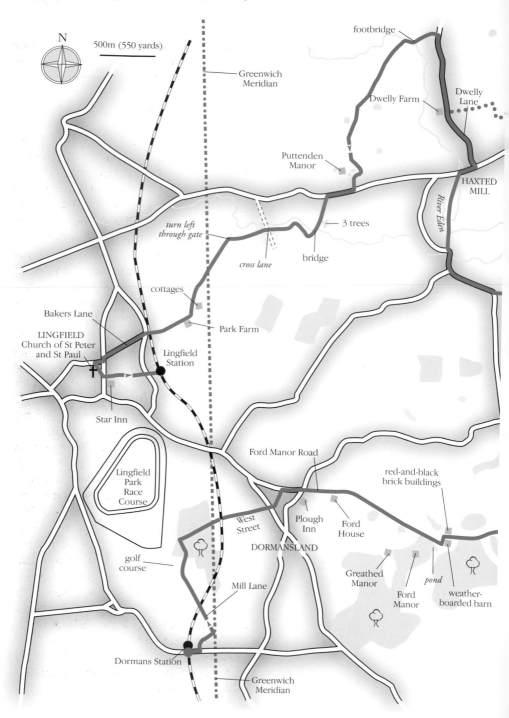

N

500m (550 yards)

Greenwich Meridian

footbridge

Dwelly Farm

Dwelly Lane

HAXTED MILL

Puttenden Manor

River Eden

3 trees

turn left through gate

cross lane

bridge

cottages

Bakers Lane

Park Farm

LINGFIELD
Church of St Peter
and St Paul

Lingfield Station

Star Inn

Ford Manor Road

red-and-black brick buildings

Lingfield Park Race Course

West Street

Plough Inn

Ford House

golf course

DORMANSLAND

Greathed Manor

pond

Ford Manor

weather-boarded barn

Mill Lane

Dormans Station

Greenwich Meridian

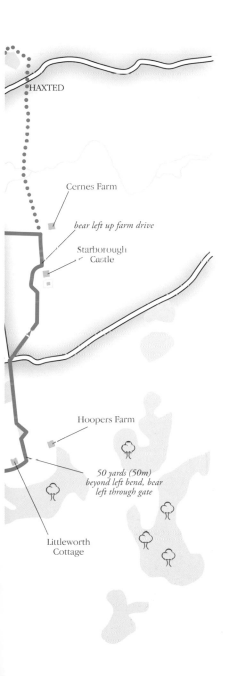

HAXTED

Cernes Farm

bear left up farm drive

Starborough Castle

Hoopers Farm

50 yards (50m) beyond left bend, bear left through gate

Littleworth Cottage

the custodianship of the captured Duc d'Orléans, father of King Louis XII. He brought the duc back with him to Starborough, the first of many country residences where the unfortunate man was to languish in feather-bedded captivity for the following 20 years. The Cobhams championed kings of England in the lists and fought for them on many battlefields.

Starborough Castle is strictly private property. Beside its gates (just after white gates) turn left over a stile (VW yellow arrow), then right along the field edge with the hedge on your right. On the far side of the property cross a stile and turn right along a lane for 50 yards (50m), then bear left (425442) up a farm drive (NB – the VW yellow arrow is badly placed here, implying that you cross a stile on your left – don't!). In 100 yards (100m) you pass a post with two yellow arrows. One points right; but follow the other VW arrow ahead towards Cernes Farm for 70 yards (70m), then turn left over a stile (426445). (*For alternative route from this point, missing out Haxted Mill but avoiding a short, nasty stretch of road, see directions in italics on page 138.*) To continue via road and Haxted Mill, follow the direction shown by the VW yellow arrow. Cross a footbridge and a stile, and keep ahead to the top left corner of the next field where you cross a stile into a road (421445) and turn right (VW sign). In 400 yards (400m) pass a single-track road on your left, and in another 50 yards (50m) cross a bridge over the Eden Brook. On the far side turn right over a stile (418447 – FP fingerpost) and go over the field (bear left following the direction of the road) to cross the River Eden by a footbridge (417450). Keep ahead between the river and Haxted millstream to reach the road at Haxted Mill (419455).

*Alternative route from Cernes Farm: Turn left over the stile at the farm entrance (VW; Tandridge Border Path/TBP). In 10 yards (10m), at a three-finger post, bear right past the farm and continue north with a hedge on your right. In the third field along, bear left over a stile (TBP), then cross a footbridge over Eden Brook and another over the River Eden (424450). Cross a private airstrip and continue up a hedged green lane to reach West Haxted Farm. At the road, turn right for 10 yards (10m); cross the road (take care!), and go over a stile. Cross the field (yellow arrow on a post) to go through a gate in the top left corner. Follow the hedge, keeping it on your right, to the next field corner; turn right here over a stile by a gate (422459). Skirt anti-clockwise round the edge of a wooded dell; through a hedge gap; on along the side of the dell, then down a hedge to the bottom left corner of the field. Bear right along the bottom side of the field with the hedge on your left; at the end of the hedge, bear left across a footbridge and follow the hedge to the road at Dwelly Farm (417460). Turn right up Dwelly Lane. Continue route as described from * (see right).*

Haxted Mill

Haxted Mill is a beautiful old building, weatherboarded and white-painted under a roof of red tiles. Its eastern half was built in 1794, but the western portion dates back to Tudor times. A sack dangles by a chain outside. Inside the four-storey watermill the cogged wooden gearwheels are in good working order. There are old mill wheels, displays on milling through the ages and such recondite items as 'hoppers', 'shoes' and

'horses' – none of which is anything like it sounds! Beside the old mill, water falls into the millpond under an ornate little bridge. The Riverside Brasserie alongside is a good spot for lunch, on the terrace beside the pool.

Leave the mill, turn left along the road for 150 yards (150m), a nasty stretch in a narrow cutting; then turn left along Dwelly Lane ('Oxted' and 'Surrey Cycleway' signs) – also a motor road, but a quieter one. Pass Haxted Kennels and Dwelly Farm. (*Alternative route rejoins here.*)

Soon the road passes through a copse. As you leave the trees, turn left through a gate (466466). Follow the fence round to the left to cross a stile in the far left corner of the field (yellow arrow). Bear left to cross a brook by a footbridge: follow the yellow arrow direction beside a fence to pass through a gap in the far hedge near a clump of trees. Keep a hedge on your left and follow the field edge. At the end of this field, go through a hedge gap (411462), and walk across the following diamond-shaped field, crossing a stile in the furthest corner. Cross the next field to the far right corner; cross the stile here (409457) and bear left along a wide path between hedges. At the bottom, follow yellow arrows to the left and around Puttenden Manor to the road (410453).

Turn right, pass one FP fingerpost on the left, and in 200 yards (200m) turn left over a stile (408453 – FP fingerpost and yellow arrow). Steer diagonally right across a field, aiming for three trees standing together a little to the left of telegraph poles. Cross Eden Brook by a bridge here (406450). On the far side bear right (yellow arrow) and follow the brook for 500 yards (500m) to go over a stile (yellow arrow) on to a lane (403450). Cross the lane and go through the gate opposite. Follow the direction of the yellow arrow to cross a ditch in a line of trees, then aim a little left across the next field towards a gate in the far hedge.

Just before you reach it, turn left through a gate in the left-hand hedge (399449). Keep forward with a hedge on your left and the spire of Lingfield church ahead and slightly to the right. At the bottom of the field go through a gate, over a stile (397445) and on along a green lane. Pass cottages on your left, then a FP fingerpost on your right. Keep ahead, and in 15 yards (15m) bear right along the front of Park Farm farmhouse (396442). Pass the gates of the farmhouse and continue along the gravelled lane to cross the railway on the level (393441) into the eastern outskirts of Lingfield. Cross a road and go down Bakers Lane opposite; at the top of the road bear left along Church Road. In 10 yards (10m) a footpath on the right of the road leads through the churchyard to the Church of St Peter and St Paul (389438).

Church of St Peter and St Paul, Lingfield

The glory of this church is its richly carved and decorated tombs and its superb brasses to members of the Cobham family. The effigy of Reginald, the 1st Lord Cobham, lies on the south side of the Lady Chapel. His head rests on a Saracen's head helm and his feet on another Saracen, a little figure dressed in a red robe and black slippers, with a comical air of frowning resignation as he shoulders Lord Cobham's enormous pointed iron shoes. The knight was the builder of Starborough Castle, and fought both at Crécy (1346) and Poitiers (1356).

Against the north wall of the Lady Chapel is the dark marble tomb of the 2nd Lord Cobham, inlaid with a wonderful elaborate brass. Brasses featuring Cobham ladies in beautiful dresses fill the chapel floor between the two knights, father and son.

In front of the high altar is the most sumptuous tomb of all, topped by the alabaster effigies of the 3rd Lord Cobham and his wife Ann Bardolf, their feet resting on a pair of curious little dragons. This Lord Cobham was one of Henry V's 'band of brothers' who fought beside him at the Battle of Agincourt in 1415. In 1431 he founded a college in Lingfield, and had the church rebuilt. It seemed one more high point in a family story of perpetual success; but within 25 years the Cobhams were extinct.

The 3rd Lord Cobham's lovely and spirited daughter Eleanor married Humphrey, Duke of Gloucester. According to William Shakespeare's *Henry VI*, Eleanor provoked a surge of jealousy in the king's wife. Eleanor was arraigned on trumped-up charges of treason and sorcery, and condemned to lifelong incarceration on the Isle of Man.

Leave the churchyard by the south-east corner, passing Church Gate Cottage to cross a road (389437). Walk down the left side of the Star Inn along a tarmac footpath that crosses open ground to reach a road (393437); cross the road to reach Lingfield Station.

19. BALCOMBE, ARDINGLY RESERVOIR & WAKEHURST PLACE

Woodlands and water dominate this lovely walk through the Wealden landscape of north Sussex. Ardingly Reservoir gives a fine waterside walk with plenty of opportunity for birdwatching, while the oak, pine and beech woods that clothe the slopes and hilltops are beautiful to walk through. There's a great story attached to the Culpeper brasses in St Peter's Church at Ardingly (pronounced 'Arding–lie'). The Culpeper family lived at nearby Wakehurst Place for centuries; the estate now forms a rural outstation of the Royal Botanic Gardens at Kew, where you can enjoy rare and beautiful plants and trees and explore the delights of the Millennium Seed Bank.

START AND FINISH:	Balcombe Station
LENGTH OF WALK:	9 miles (14km)
OS MAPS:	1:50,000 Landranger 187; 1:25,000 Explorer 135
TRAVEL:	By rail from London King's Cross (1 hr) or London Bridge (40 mins); by road – M25 (Jct 7/8), M23 (Jct 10a), B2036.
FEATURES:	Ardingly Reservoir (bring binoculars for bird-watching); Culpeper and Wakehurst brasses in St Peter's Church, Ardingly; Wakehurst Place Royal Botanic Gardens and Tudor mansion and Millennium Seed Bank; woodlands of the Sussex Weald.
REFRESHMENTS:	Balcombe Tea Rooms and Half Moon PH, Balcombe; Wakehurst Place Restaurant.

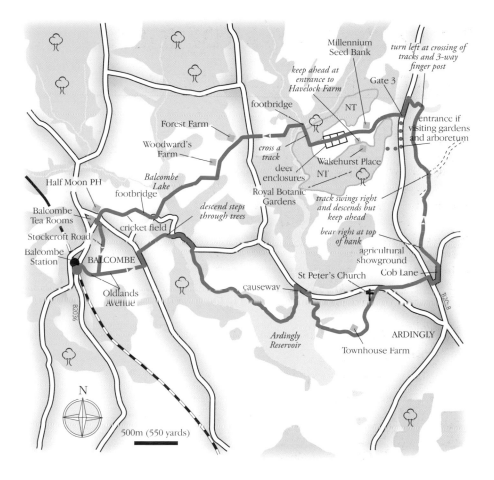

From Balcombe Station (307301) climb steps and cross the B2036 beside a telephone box. Climb the path and bear right along residential Oldlands Avenue for ½ mile (0.75km) to a T-junction (315302). Turn left, and in 150 yards (150m) go right across a stile (concrete BW marker). Cross another stile and follow the path over a field and down by the right side of a wood. At the bottom corner of the wood pass a BW fingerpost on your left, and in 10 yards (10m) turn left through a gate and descend steps through the trees to a road (318305). Turn right to cross the 'wrist' of Ardingly Reservoir's western arm. Follow the road uphill for 200 yards (200m), then turn right through a gate (319304 – BW fingerpost and Ardingly Reservoir notice). Descend to the water's edge and bear left along the margin of the reservoir.

141

Ardingly Reservoir

The V-shaped system of valleys between Balcombe and Ardingly was flooded in 1977 to create this big artificial lake. Ardingly is a particularly beautiful reservoir with a curving shoreline, reed and wetland areas, and thickly wooded banks. The trees are mainly larch, pine and silver birch, with patches of older hazel coppice and sweet chestnut. By the water grow small oaks and willows. Warblers and other songbirds thrive in the woods, while the big sheet of water is a natural magnet for waterbirds – coots, moorhens, great crested grebe and other divers, along with Canada geese in big flocks, cormorants and herons fishing the shallows. Birdwatching hides stand out in the water on stalky legs – so don't forget your binoculars!

Follow the shore path for $1^1/_3$ miles (2km) to reach a road (331299), where you turn right to cross the eastern arm of the reservoir by a causeway. On the far side turn right through a kissing gate (FP fingerpost) and continue along the waterside footpath. On the far side of the second bay turn left over a stile (333295 – FP fingerpost) and climb the slope to cross another stile (FP fingerpost). Walk up the field with a hedge on your left. At the top, cross a stile and continue along a lane (at first deeply rutted) that leads past Townhouse Farm (338293) before curving left to run up to St Peter's Church at Ardingly (340298).

The Culpeper Abductions

St Peter's is a 14th-century church of grey and yellow stone with a squat, sturdy tower and a timber porch. Beneath an ornate tabernacle against the north wall of the sanctuary is an altar tomb that holds a fine brass to Sir Richard Wakehurst (d. 1434) and his wife Elizabeth. Under the chancel aisle carpet are four more beautiful brasses, two of them commemorating brothers Nicholas and Richard Culpeper. 'Nichas' is shown in armour beside his wife Elizabeth, who wears a long headdress and an elaborately embroidered girdle, while 'Ric' Culpeper lies by his wife Margarete.

The brothers did not gain their ladies through gentle courtship. Elizabeth and Margarete Wakehurst were heiresses to the Wakehurst lands and fortunes, and orphans – a nice catch for 'a pair of ruthless fortune hunters', as the Culpeper brothers have been labelled. On the death of their father, the girls were placed under the protection of Sir John Culpeper, elder brother to Nicholas and Richard; but that did not prevent the young men turning up fully armed to abduct the heiresses. Amid 'great and piteous lamentation and weeping', Elizabeth and Margarete were forcibly

Opposite: The handsome Tudor mansion of Wakehurst Place stands at the centre of wonderful gardens. These gardens are maintained by the Royal Botanic Gardens of Kew as an environment where many rare and delicate plant species can flourish in sheltered conditions.

removed and forthwith married to the brothers. As things turned out, Margarete died childless; but Nicholas and Elizabeth Culpeper produced 10 sons and 8 daughters, whose stiff little images you can see etched into the brass below their parents.

At the T-junction by St Peter's, turn right along the road; then in 10 yards (10m) bear left (FP fingerpost) down a track. In 50 yards (50m) go through a gate and turn right on a tarmac track along the south edge of the South of England Agricultural Showground. At the B2028 (346300) turn right for 100 yards (100m); cross with care, and turn left down Cob Lane. In 300 yards (300m) bear left (347301 – BW fingerpost) up a woodland track. At the top of the bank bear right (345303 – BW fingerpost) through the woods, losing height gradually. In ¹/₂ mile (0.75km) a stony trackway comes in from the left; then in 100 yards (100m) a BW fingerpost points you on ahead. In another 20 yards (20m) the trackway swings right and descends steeply (346311); but keep ahead here.

In another ¹/₂ mile (0.75km), you reach a crossing of tracks (346319) at a three-way BW fingerpost, with a gateway to a house drive on your right. Turn left here along a track. In 50 yards (50m) the track divides, take the left fork (BW fingerpost). In another 50 yards (50m) branch to the right (BW fingerpost) on a narrow track that climbs to the B2028 (344320). Cross the road and turn left along the grass verge for 300 yards (300m) until you reach Gate 3 entrance to the grounds

of Wakehurst Place. If you want to visit the gardens and arboretum, continue along the road verge for approximately 250 yards (250m) to turn right across a car park to the ticket kiosk and entrance.

Wakehurst Place

Sir Edward Culpeper built the mansion of Wakehurst Place in 1590, by which time the ancient Kent and Sussex family was already in decline from its medieval heyday. Later Culpepers got themselves into financial fixes – one even had to sell the entire estate for £9,000 to cover his gambling debts. In 1903, the amateur but expert botanist Sir Gerald Loder bought Wakehurst Place, and created 170 acres (70ha) of superb gardens over the following 30 years. In 1963, the house, gardens and woodlands – along with £200,000 – were given to the National Trust by the then owner, menswear millionaire Sir Henry Price of 'Fifty Shilling Tailors' fame. The NT lease the property to the Royal Botanic Gardens at Kew, which runs it as an outstation.

The dry, sandy soil of north Sussex succours species that might not do so well on the damp London clay of Kew – here the climate is milder, the air cleaner and the situation more sheltered. A collection of shrubs and trees of world importance has been built up at Wakehurst. The tree collection, one of the finest in Britain, features exotics from the Himalaya, North America, the Mediterranean and both the Near and Far East, as well as the native oaks, pines and beeches that have been retained. The plant collection has been planned to give spectacular shows throughout the year, from daffodil sheets in spring through cottage-garden plants and orchids in summer to a winter garden full of scented and coloured plants and scrub trees. There's also a superb mosaic of habitat in the 150-acre (60-ha) Loder Valley Reserve, an area carefully managed for the benefit of badgers, deer, dormice and other animals, birds and insects native to the Sussex Weald.

Millennium Seed Bank

Outside the perimeter of the National Trust property is the Millennium Seed Bank, housed in barrel-roofed glasshouses that look like ultra-modern versions of Victorian train sheds. This is an exciting international project to collect, freeze and preserve the seed of up to 24,000 plant species from all over the world. You can stroll around the cases displaying seeds with the appearance of abstract sculpture, seeds huge and tiny, fossil seeds and seeds arranged like artistic installations. Behind glass screens the Seed Bank's scientists go about their work of preserving, germinating, propagating and cataloguing the seeds, seemingly indifferent to the fascinated onlookers.

If you are not visiting the arboretum and gardens, turn right off the B2028 through Gate 3, and follow the drive past the Millennium Seed Bank (340317). Follow the footpath (FP fingerpost) down the left side of the Seed Bank. At the entrance of Havelock Farm (338316) keep ahead on a gravelly track between fences. In 50 yards (50m) pass through a kissing gate (FP fingerpost) and continue along a path between deer-fences and through deer-gates, to cross a stile into the woods (333315).

Woods Around Wakehurst

These woods form the southern remnants of the Forest of Worth, which, together with St Leonard's Forest, draped a vast blanket of trees across the High Weald of Sussex in medieval times. In the Tudor era, yeomen farmers were felling trees and cutting farms out of the heathland and wildwood, and by the 18th century the forest was greatly diminished. Nevertheless, there are still plenty of beautiful beeches, oaks, sweet chestnuts and ash trees, and a scatter of hammer ponds as a reminder of the medieval ironworking industry that enriched local ironmasters and polluted the countryside.

As you enter the woods bear right downhill (FP fingerpost). In 100 yards (100m) cross a track at a two-finger FP fingerpost and keep ahead along the footpath, through a tall kissing gate and on down to cross a footbridge. In 50 yards (50m) turn left (332317 – FP fingerpost) to cross two more streams and climb to the edge of the wood. Leave the wood, bearing left through a wooden gate (331317). Turn left and follow the wood edge, bending right to continue for 1/4 mile (0.4km) and cross a stile into a road (326315). Turn right for 10 yards (10m), then left along a stony lane ('Forest Farm' sign and FP fingerpost). In 150 yards (150m) the lane swings right towards Forest Farm; keep ahead here (FP fingerpost) to continue with a hedge on your left. Cross a stile at the bottom of the field (323313) and bear diagonally left across the next field, following the FP fingerpost direction. Cross the stile on the far side (FP fingerpost) and turn right along the top of the next field to cross a stile and turn left along a farm lane (321311).

Follow the lane to meet a road and cross over the foot of Balcombe Lake. In 40 yards (40m) turn right over a stile (315307) to cross the bottom of a field, then a footbridge. Bear left for 10 yards (10m) until you reach an oak tree, and follow the line of four trees up the slope to meet a hedge at the crest of the field. Turn left at the fingerpost and follow the hedge, keeping it on your right, to go through a kissing gate. Follow the hedge up to the top left corner of the field, and bear left with a hedge on your right to go through a kissing gate and along a track. Follow it across a cricket field and through a hedge gap into a lane (312307). Turn right to reach a crossroads in Balcombe (309307). Cross, and walk along Bramble Hill for 30 yards (30m); turn left opposite Balcombe Tea Rooms along Stockcroft Road for $^1/_3$ mile (0.5km) to Oldlands Avenue (309301). Turn right here to return to Balcombe Station.

20. POLESDEN LACEY & RANMORE COMMON

Beautiful woods on the shoulders of the Surrey downs, sweeping views across two deep valleys, a great country house and a stretch of England's oldest road – these are some of the delights of this walk. It explores a well-favoured corner of the North Downs, preserved for the enjoyment of all by a curious mixture of private generosity and public farsightedness. At centre stage stands Polesden Lacey, a classic English country house, where the spirit of sharp-tongued Edwardian hostess Mrs Ronald Greville still rules the roost. A highlight of the house, now in the care of the National Trust, is its three-sided Picture Corridor hung with dozens of 17th-century Dutch landscapes and other Old Master paintings. Moving from this hothouse of social manners and artifice through the tangled wildwood of Ranmore Common to tread the ancient North Downs Way in the footsteps of Bronze Age traders offers a pleasingly steep set of contrasts.

START AND FINISH:	Boxhill and Westhumble Station
LENGTH OF WALK:	9 miles (14km)
OS MAPS:	1:50,000 Landranger 187; 1:25,000 Explorer 146
TRAVEL:	By rail from London Victoria or London Waterloo (46 mins); by road – M25 (Jct 9), A24.
FEATURES:	Fanny Burney plaque at Westhumble; Norbury Park estate and house; Polesden Lacey (NT); Ranmore Common (NT); North Downs Way; St Bartholomew's Church; Westhumble Chapel ruin (NT).
REFRESHMENTS:	Stepping Stones PH, Westhumble; Polesden Lacey tea room.

Boxhill and Westhumble railway station (167518) is a fine example of the lengths that Victorian railway companies went to in order to impress and flatter their customers. The pillar capitals and corbels of the porch at the little halt on the Leatherhead–Dorking line were furnished with fine carvings of fruit and flowers, which still enchant those who use the station.

N

500m (550 yards)

GREAT
BOOKHAM

A246

A246

Admiral's Road

entrance to
Polesden Lacey

Polesden Lacey house

thatched bridge
orchard

yew avenue

Yewtree Farm

Ranmore Common

Steers Field

cross the road

join North Downs Way

North Downs Way

Philgrim's Way

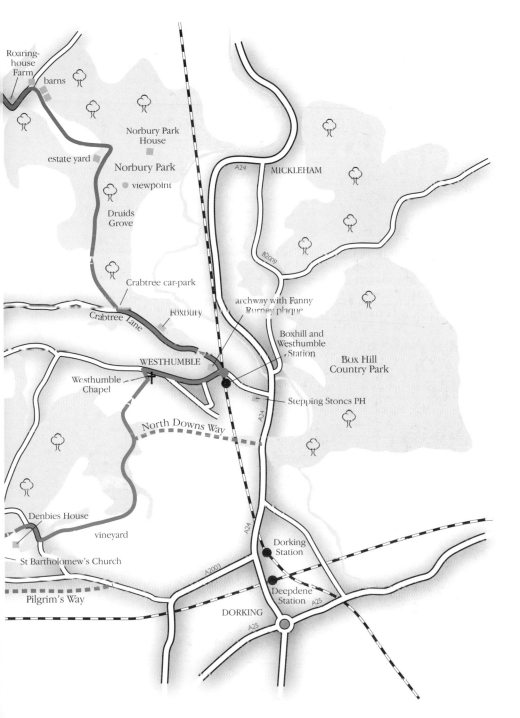

Roaring-house Farm

barns

Norbury Park House

estate yard

Norbury Park

viewpoint

Druids Grove

Crabtree car-park

Crabtree Lane

Foxbury

WESTHUMBLE

Westhumble Chapel

North Downs Way

Denbies House

vineyard

St Bartholomew's Church

Pilgrim's Way

A24

MICKLEHAM

B2009

archway with Fanny Burney plaque

Boxhill and Westhumble Station

Box Hill Country Park

Stepping Stones PH

A24

Dorking Station

Deepdene Station

A2003

DORKING

A25

A25

Fanny Burney and Westhumble

Leaving the station, make for the large flint and stone archway ahead. Its blue plaque records the residence in Westhumble of celebrated Georgian novelist and diarist Fanny Burney and her husband, the French exile General d'Arblay. The bubbly Fanny had published her novel *Camilla* in 1796, and was in demand as a guest. She had made great friends with the Locke family of nearby Norbury Park, and it was they who gave her land at Westhumble on which to build 'Camilla Cottage'. On the day in 1797 that Fanny and her husband moved in, the impetuous general went 'striding over hedge and ditch' in his hurry to get to the new house – which was completely unfurnished, containing only 'a glorious fire of wood, and a little bench, borrowed of one of the carpenters: nothing else'. The couple were happy enough in Camilla Cottage, however, as they walked, socialised and gardened – the general once dug up an entire asparagus bed under the impression that it was a patch of weeds.

From the archway, bear right along Crabtree Lane, with views to your right of the white bulk of Norbury Park House on its sweep of green lawns in a clearing in the woods. Pass 'Foxbury' on your right, and in another ¼ mile (0.5km) bear right through Crabtree car park (158525 –

PB). Continue along the western edge of the wood on a bridleway, which soon becomes a surfaced track.

Norbury Park Estate

Surrey County Council bought up the 1,300 acres (520ha) of the Norbury Park Estate in 1930, an act of farsightedness that saved this mosaic of farmland, chalk grassland and woodland from housing development. The bridleway you are following is just one of many that run through mixed woodland of beech, ash and cherry – trees highly characteristic of these flinty chalk downs – along with maple, sycamore and hazel coppice. Blackbirds, tits and warblers thrive in these woods, and you may hear the scutter of squirrels and occasional crash of a roe deer breaking through the undergrowth. Primroses and bluebells do well under the trees and along the paths in spring, but none grows in the cold shade of Druids Grove (157533). Here you'll find ancient yews with iron-hard limbs, some of them perhaps 2,000 years old. Beyond the grove a signposted viewpoint just to the east of the bridleway gives superb views out from the trees across the valley of the River Mole to Juniper Hill. Away to the right stands the dark, tree-cloaked rise of Box Hill, the favourite 1950s and '60s Bank Holiday destination of London's motorbikers.

Opposite: From the open flank of Box Hill there are sweeping views across the low-lying Wealden landscape, which is thickly wooded and patched by hedges into countless squares of brown and green.

When the trees are not in full leaf there are glimpses to the left of the large conservatories and white, many-windowed walls of Norbury Park House (160537). The house was built in 1774 for the Locke family, friends and benefactors of Fanny Burney. By then the estate had already been stripped of much of its woodland, its beautiful walnut trees having been sold to make musket stocks for the Army. In 1890, Norbury Park was bought by Leopold Salmon – he also bought Box Hill and presented it to the National Trust. The house's most famous 20th-century inhabitant was Dr Marie Stopes, brave and controversial pioneer of family planning clinics, who lived here until her death in 1957.

Back on the track, continue north to pass a timber yard on your left. Just beyond, bear left at a picnic place (158538) to follow a good stony bridleway out of the trees on to open/common land. Here there are three tracks to follow. Take the middle one straight over the heath and follow it until you come to a PB post and junction of paths. Head left for the splendid old tiled and weatherboarded barn at Roaringhouse Farm (149541).

Turn right here up a track for 300 yards (300m) to the crest of the ridge, then go left ('Public Byway' fingerpost) along a track called Admiral's Road, with fine roof-of-the-downs views all round. The new houses of Great Bookham, crowding almost up to Admiral's Road, are a sharp reminder of how much walkers owe the previous generations who fought to maintain these downs in their green and wooded state.

In ¹/₃ mile (0.5km) keep ahead at a crossing of paths (148539) along a hedged lane to cross Dorking Road/Chapel Lane (141533). Keep ahead along Polesden Road (brown 'Polesden Lacey' sign) on a footpath on the right side of the road for 1/3 mile (0.5km) to the arched entrance to Polesden Lacey on the left (137527). NB If not visiting Polesden Lacey, keep ahead here, bearing left in 200 yards (200m) where the road splits (following the sign for Yewtree Farm), along the west side of the property to rejoin the route at the top of a yew avenue (133521 – see page 154 at *).

Polesden Lacey

For a country house with such a grand reputation Polesden Lacey (136522) stands surprisingly low, a two-storey building in cheerful yellow and white, its two wings running forward to end in pretty bow fronts. A central clock tower rises in the middle of the ensemble. 'Polesdene' appears in written records going back nearly 700 years, but the current house dates to an 1824 rebuild of the Polesden Lacey that a former owner, dramatist Richard Brinsley Sheridan, thought 'the nicest place, within a prudent distance of London, in England'. Sheridan bought the estate in 1797, the year that Fanny Burney moved into Camilla Cottage just down the road. He made a terraced walk, set up a good library and installed his beloved second wife. 'It shall be', he promised, 'a seat of health and happiness where she shall chirp like a bird, bound like a fawn and grow fat as a little pig.'

The Hon. Mrs Ronald Greville certainly chirped like a bird when she was in residence in the early 20th century, shooting her famed and feared poison darts of malicious wit among the kings and queens, dukes and duchesses who filled her drawing room and gathered round her extremely well-appointed dining table. And, by all accounts, it was Mrs Greville's butler Bacon who grew fat as a little pig on a steady clandestine intake of his employer's delicacies and fine wines. Mrs Greville loved a lord, and a monarch even more. King Edward VII came to stay, Queen Mary was a friend, and as for the Duke and Duchess of York (later King George VI and Queen Elizabeth) – Mrs Greville appointed herself a kind of honorary favourite aunt to the young couple, who honeymooned at Polesden Lacey in 1923. The mettlesome hostess ('Maggie Greville! I would sooner have an open sewer in my drawing room!' – Lady Leslie) filled Polesden Lacey with fine pictures, porcelain, furniture and silver.

Truth to tell, Maggie Greville was no better than she ought to have been. She was the illegitimate daughter of a rich Scottish brewer and his lover, the wife of the brewery's day porter. Maggie used to say, 'I'd rather be a beeress than an heiress,' but she grew up to court and respect money, power

and position. In the 1930s, along with several of her contemporaries, she became an admirer of Nazism. She had an acid tongue, and could be a formidable enemy. But she was also generous and warm-hearted, one of life's radiators. When she died in 1942 she left Polesden Lacey to the National Trust with the wish that it should always be open to the public – not the sentiments of an unregenerate snob, as she is sometimes painted.

In the picture corridor at Polesden Lacey there is a telling portrait of Mrs Greville painted in 1891 at the time of her marriage – a vivacious, humorous-looking young beauty with sparkling black eyes, warm in her fur cloak. Take your time strolling around the corridor – many wonderful paintings are hung on the dark panelled walls. Notable are the 17th-century Dutch canal scenes and seascapes such as Aert van der Neer's wintry skaters in *A Town on a Frozen River*, the coastal landscape and inshore shipping in *The Zuider Zee Coast near Muiden* by Jacob van Ruisdael, and a mournful bull beside a lake by bovine specialist Aelbert Cuyp. The drawing room is smothered in gold leaf and Green Men, beautiful hand-painted Meissen porcelain adorns the study, and in the smoking room there is a gaggle of royal photographs including King Edward VII (his signature is the first in the Polesden Lacey visitors' book on display), the Prince of Thurn and Taxis, the Maharajah of Cooch Behar and Alice Keppel, Edward VII's ripe peach of a mistress.

There are 30 acres (12ha) of Edwardian gardens to explore before you make your departure from Polesden Lacey by way of the walled garden and a thatched bridge over a sunken lane to the west of the house. Go diagonally left from the bridge to the bottom left-hand corner of the orchard beyond (132522); at the gate turn sharp left along the wood edge. In 200 yards (200m) go through a gate to the top of the yew avenue (133521 – * alternative route rejoins here). Do not take the surfaced lane ahead ('Polesden Farm' sign), but turn right downhill (blue arrow) on a raised causeway through the yew avenue. Turn right at the bridleway and pass Yewtree Farm (132516); then continue ahead (south) on a fine flinty track, keeping straight ahead through the woods on Ranmore Common for ³/₄ mile (1.25km).

Ranmore Common

For centuries Ranmore Common was open heath where local commoners had the right to graze their animals. Once domestic economies no longer relied on the house cow, pig or goose, the common quickly became overgrown with scrub. Now it is a broad, loose-knit wood of oak, yew, holly and birch, famous for bluebells in early summer and protected by the National Trust.

The section of bridleway shown on the maps running due south between OS grid reference 132509 and the road at OS grid reference 132504 has vanished among the trees. Simply keep ahead on the obvious track through the wood to cross the road in a dip (133504). Turn right for 250 yards (250m), then bear left down a broad woodland ride (notice prohibiting motorbikes, cars and horse-drawn wagons). In 300 yards (300m) turn left along the North Downs Way at OS grid reference 132500.

North Downs Way

This beautiful old flinty trackway, the oldest road in England, has been hammered out by the tread of beasts and men over at least 5,000 years – maybe much more. It keeps a sheltered and concealed course just below the crests of the ridges and hills. In all it runs for 250 miles (400km), under various guises and names, from Devon to Kent. The eastern half of the trackway between Farnham in Surrey and the Kentish coast is designated the North Downs Way National Trail. Another ancient trackway, the Pilgrims' Way from Winchester, runs in the valley just below Ranmore Common. Medieval pilgrims in their millions – including Geoffrey Chaucer's *Canterbury Tales* travellers – trod or rode the Pilgrims' Way to the shrine of St Thomas à Becket in Canterbury Cathedral. For some stretches it interweaves with the North Downs Way ridge track. Some call the ancient ridgeway the Harrow Way, or Hoary Way – the Old Road. Bronze Age tin merchants probably used it; so did traders, drovers, warriors and packhorsemen. Now its sole use is as a leisure footpath and bridleway, a beautiful old grandstand for views such as the one you enjoy as you walk – across the valley and wooded downs, over the roofs, towers and spires of Dorking.

Entering Steers Field (140503), do not aim for the church spire ahead, but steer slightly to the right of it, keeping the contour for 200 yards (200m); then follow NDW signs to a road (143504). Cross, following the 'Parish Church' sign, to pass St Bartholomew's Church on your right (146505). It was built in 1850 by Thomas Cubitt, builder of much of Victorian London. Cubitt faced St Bartholomew's strikingly in round flint cobbles, and did not neglect to add a tremendous spire that soon acquired the nickname of 'Cubitt's Finger'. Inside, a dignified little chapel is a memorial to the three sons of Lord and Lady Ashcombe – the brothers were all killed during the First World War.

Continue along the road from the church. In ¹/₃ mile (0.5km), where the road bends left outside the gates of Denbies House (151506), keep ahead; in 30 yards (30m) turn right (NDW fingerpost), then left along the North Downs Way (you'll find the fingerpost to the right-hand side of the track, opposite the entrance). Pass through large estate gates, ignoring the 'Private' sign, and keep the contour along a steep hillside above the Denbies vineyard – a fairly recent venture on this south-facing slope. There is a great view ahead to Box Hill rising high on the horizon.

Keep ahead, ignoring a 'Woodland Walk' track to the left immediately after a second set of gates, to enter woods (158507). Cross a bridlepath (158512); in 250 yards (250m) the North Downs Way bears downhill to the right (159514), but bear left here (FP fingerpost). In 300 yards (300m) bear right along a drive, down to the road by Westhumble Chapel.

Westhumble Chapel

A flint-built west gable with a crude circular central window and a narrow upper window accounts for most of what is left of the little chapel founded for the Westhumble villagers in the late 12th century. By the time of the Reformation it was already disused. At various times it saw service as a barn, and when the railway was being built in the 19th century, the chapel saw congregations once more in the rough forms of the railway navvies.

From the chapel, turn right along the road to reach Boxhill and Westhumble Station.

21. SHERE, THE NORTH DOWNS WAY, ST MARTHA-ON-THE-HILL & THE PILGRIMS' WAY

Two ancient trackways run east-west along the valley of the Tilling Bourne, their parallel courses ½ mile (0.75km) apart – the old droving route that now carries the North Downs Way National Trail high along the chalk ridge of the North Downs and the Pilgrims' Way track through the valley at the feet of the downs. Heading out west along the high road and coming back by the low road, your walk is bookended by notable churches. You'll visit 'Surrey's prettiest village' in Shere – a title you may well think justified. There are fabulous far views from Newlands Corner high on the downs and a poignant old fable based around the limpid waters of Silent Pool in the valley below. Add beautiful woodland and meadows, and you have a truly delectable walk in prospect.

START AND FINISH: Gomshall Station

LENGTH OF WALK: 10½ miles (17km)

OS MAPS: 1:50,000 Landranger 187; 1:25,000 Explorer 145

TRAVEL: By rail from London Waterloo (1 hr); by road – M25 (Jct 10), A3, A247, A25.

FEATURES: St James's Church and the village of Shere; North Downs Way ancient trackway; views from Newlands Corner; Church of St Martha-on-the-Hill; Pilgrims' Way ancient trackway; Silent Pool; Catholic and Apostolic Church, Albury.

REFRESHMENTS: White Horse PH, Shere; New Barn Coffee Shop, Newlands Corner.

From Gomshall Station (089478), exit either side. Cross the A25 and go under the railway line to turn right down Wonham Way. Keep ahead for 250 yards (250m), crossing a stream, and at the sharp left bend turn right (087475; 'Cycle Route 22' sign). In another 250 yards (250m) pass under the railway again. Bear left along the lane to a crossroads (082476); go across into Gravelpits Lane, and in 100 yards (100m) bear right by Gravelpits Farm house into a lane going west across fields. In $1/3$ mile (0.5km) turn right through a gate (076477) to reach St James's Church in Shere (074478).

St James's Church and Shere Village

St James's Church is a beautiful Norman building. The lychgate was designed by Sir Edwin Lutyens, perfectly framing the Norman tower under its broach spire. A heavy old gallery at the west end is the prelude to a plain, whitewashed interior. There is some lovely 14th-century glass – hawks, animals and foliage – and a really exquisite tiny 13th-century statuette of the Virgin and Child in bronze, which was retrieved by chance from a bramble bush by a dog. It might have been part of a crozier, or perhaps it fell from the staff of some medieval penitent travelling the Pilgrims' Way through the village.

Behind the altar are traces of 12th-century fresco – foliage and tracery in red ochre round one of the window splays. A little 14th-century quatrefoil window in the chancel was inserted so that the Anchoress of Shere, Christine Carpenter, could view the saying of the Mass. This holy nun was incarcerated in a narrow cell in the church wall at her own request in 1329. She forced her way out at one point, to 'run about, being torn to pieces by attacks of the Tempter'. But after sorrowfully petitioning the bishop of Winchester to be allowed to resume her vocation, she was locked up in prayerful isolation in her cramped cell once more.

Shere is a gorgeous village, threaded by the sparklingly clear Tilling Bourne stream, its lanes lined with fascinating old houses. Look for Bill and Ben the Flowerpot Men in a cottage garden, the old brick-and-flint village lock-up with its barred window overlooking the stream, and any number of crooked houses of great charm.

From the church, walk forward to turn right opposite the White Horse pub. Turn left at the T-junction (073479), and in 20 yards (20m) turn right up the side of Shere recreation ground. Go under the A25, and bear immediately left up a zigzag path, then right on a track up the left side of Netley Plantation for $1/2$ mile (0.75km) to Hollister Farm (073490). After the farm the track forks; don't turn left, but keep straight ahead uphill to reach a road at the crest of the downs (072494). Turn right along the road for a few yards (take care, sharp corner!); then bear left along the North Downs Way National Trail/NDW, and follow it for $1^3/4$ miles (2.75km) to Newlands Corner (044492).

North Downs Way: The Old Road to Newlands Corner

The North Downs Way (see pages 105–12 and 147–55) bears the slithery boot-sole prints of modern-day secular pilgrims who tramp this ancient route for pleasure. The Way lies along the course of the oldest road in Britain, the

Hoary ('Ancient') or Harrow Way, used by drovers and itinerant traders for many millennia before Thomas à Becket's sainthood drew religious penitents to Canterbury. This is a wide old road with broad verges, snaking through dark groves of yew and holly at the top of the downs, keeping just to the south of the crest, combining maximum shelter and view with minimum exposure to unfriendly eyes. Things are quiet along the old road, with very little noise unless a high wind is rushing through the beech tops.

At Newlands Corner, a junction of road and greens, enormous views open out – south across the Tilling Bourne valley and the greensand hills of Surrey and Sussex towards the South Downs and north over chalk downland slopes into the low-lying clay basin of London and the Thames Valley. There must be 50 miles (80km) of country in view. Chalkhill flowers, butterflies and birds abound, thanks to the conservation policy of letting sheep and cattle graze this open grassland.

Cross over the road on to Newlands Corner, and follow NDW signs across open downland for 3/4 mile (1.25km) to cross White Lane (033490), and turn left downhill on a path alongside the lane. At the bottom of the lane keep ahead by a black-and-white cottage (034486), following NDW signs through the wood. Keep ahead until you reach a broad track with a Second World War pillbox on your left. Here, turn right (032484) on a broad track marked with 'chapel logo' waymarks that climbs St Martha's Hill to the chapel on the summit (028483).

St Martha-on-the-Hill

The cruciform church, built of rough chunks of dark clinkery ironstone with yellow sandstone facings, stands among dark pine trees at the very summit of its ironstone knoll, a sombre monument. Fragments of the Norman structure built in honour of St Thomas à Becket can still be made out. The church's dedication to St Martha, the only such dedication in Britain, is probably a centuries-old corruption of 'Martyr's Chapel'. But maybe 'martyr' does not refer to St Thomas at all; there is an account of 600 early Christians being massacred for their faith here. Some say that Martha herself, sister of Mary Magdalene, visited the hill in the company of her brother Lazarus and Joseph of Arimathea. Joseph, a devout follower of Christ, was almost certainly a Phoenician tin trader who might well have known of the Harrow Way. He may even have been Jesus's uncle. Some stories tell of a journey he made to England, bringing his young nephew with him. And did those feet, in ancient time, walk upon England's mountains green...?

Opposite: The Norman Church of St James in Shere operated as a resting station, waymark and place of physical and spiritual refreshment for medieval pilgrims making their way to the shrine of St Thomas à Becket at Canterbury.

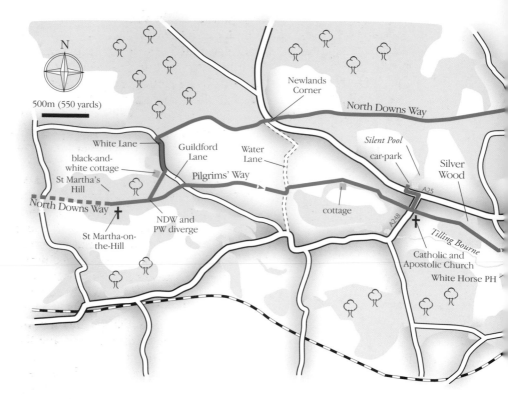

From the church retrace your steps to pass the point where the NDW branches off to the left (032484). From this point on you are following the Surrey Wildlife Trust's 'self-guided trail' (purple 'ox-head' markers/SDW (South Downs Way)) along the ancient Pilgrim's Way/PW.

Pilgrims' Way

Though the pilgrims travelling to and from Canterbury tended to use the ancient Harrow Way track, they preferred, where possible, to do what their distant ancestors could not safely do – travel along the valley floors, where there was more shelter from the weather and more water. Settlements with their promise of provisions, beds and warm inns were thicker on the ground, too. The old track just up the slope from the Tilling Bourne was probably in use long before the pilgrims began to pass through the valley, but they certainly used it in their thousands, year by year.

From the NDW junction, keep ahead along the Pilgrims' Way. In 30 yards (30m) pass an old Second World War pillbox defensive emplacement, and steer ahead. In 200

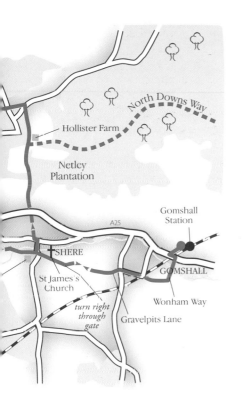

Catholic and Apostolic Church, Albury

This grand, overblown church with its pinnacles, big octagonal chapel, imposing north porch and tall graceful windows is, sadly, disused and decaying. It was built in the 1840s for Henry Drummond of Albury Park, who had joined an extreme Christian sect known as the Catholic and Apostolic Faith. The sect was founded by Drummond's charismatic friend Edward Irving, a magnetic presence who believed that the Second Coming of Christ was about to take place. Irving would preach and prophesy for hours on end to congregations of thousands in his Regent Square chapel in London. The squire of Albury fell deeply under his spell. Eventually the hellfire preacher was tried for heresy, and the Catholic and Apostolic Faith fizzled out.

Turn left up the A248 (there is a footpath on the right side of the hedge) to reach the A25, where you turn left for 100 yards (100m) to cross the dual carriageway (take great care!) into a car park. A path leads from here to Sherbourne Pond and Silent Pool (061486).

The Legend of Silent Pool

This beautiful clear pool, fed by chalk springs and romantically overhung by trees, is the setting for a legend of innocence betrayed, voyeurism and death by drowning. On a lovely day in 1193, young Emma, the woodcutter's beautiful daughter, was enjoying a naked bathe in Silent Pool. Unknown to the maiden, she was being spied on

yards (200m), at a marker post with SDW, dragonfly and other waymarks (035485), bear left to a car park and Guildford Lane. Turn right, and in 50 yards (50m) turn left (SDW waymark and BW fingerpost) along the Pilgrims' Way for ²/₃ mile (1km). Cross Water Lane (047484 – SDW and BW blue arrow) and continue on the Pilgrims' Way for ¹/₃ mile (0.5km) to a cottage (053485). Bear right here; follow the SDW through the trees along a trail, crossing a road near an old sandpit (056484) to reach the A248 (060482) just opposite the Catholic and Apostolic Church, Albury.

by wicked Prince John, who had come to see for himself if rumours of her beauty were true. Suddenly Emma became aware of the watching figure. Abashed, she waded deeper into the pool to conceal her nakedness and disappeared beneath the water. Her brother arrived, jumped in to try to save her and they drowned in each other's arms. Emma haunts the pool on moonlit nights, when she may be seen bathing and heard to scream as she slips beneath the water.

The legend of Silent Pool is not quite as old as it sounds: it was made up in Victorian times by local doggerel-scribbler Martin Turner. But there is another tale involving the royal rogue John that seems to ring a little more true. The story says that in his youth he stole the girlfriend of Stephen Langton, a youth who lived near Silent Pool. The cuckolded lover had his revenge many years later in 1215, when, as Cardinal Langton, he was one of those who stripped King John of many of his powers by forcing him to sign the first Bill of Rights, Magna Carta.

From Silent Pool return to the Pilgrims' Way. Follow it across the A248, crossing a stile to continue left and upwards across a field into Silver Wood (kissing gate). Leave the wood (066480) to cross a field and go through a windbreak of trees to reach a lane (069478). Cross the lane, and continue along the path that leads in ¹/₃ mile (0.5km) to the crossroads beside the White Horse pub in Shere. From here, retrace your steps to Gomshall Station.

22. BETCHWORTH, BROCKHAM, BUCKLAND & THE RIVER MOLE VALLEY

The three neighbouring villages of Betchworth, Brockham and Buckland sit tight together in the valley of the River Mole, surrounded by gently rolling Surrey farmland and overlooked by the green and white chalk rampart of the North Downs. Walking the farm tracks and lanes of this quiet countryside you'll find traditional village greens and duck ponds, cosy pubs, handsome old farmhouses and a scattering of woods, all tucked away in the broad flat vale of the slow-flowing River Mole.

START AND FINISH: Betchworth station

LENGTH OF WALK: 9 miles (14km)

OS MAPS: 1:50,000 Landranger 187; 1:25,000 Explorer 146

TRAVEL: By rail from London Bridge or London Victoria (1 hr approx., change at Redhill); by road – M25 (Jct 8), A217 to Reigate, A25 Dorking road.

FEATURES: Betchworth forge; Brockham village green; community village shop, Strood Green; flowery sunken lane near Rice Bridge; Buckland Deli & Gifts village shop, village green and pond.

REFRESHMENTS: Red Lion PH, Betchworth; The Dolphin, Betchworth; village shop, Buckland.

Come out of the station (main entrance), cross the road and climb steps (fingerpost, slightly obscured, by level-crossing lights) along a fenced footpath at the edge of the railway cutting, until you descend to turn right through a kissing gate into a field. Keep right of a house and walk down the field, aiming for a gap in the far hedge. Cross a rough footbridge and turn right along the field edge (yellow arrow) with the hedge on your right. Cross a stile in the far corner (yellow arrow) and follow a fenced path along the back of houses between a fence and a ditch. Climb steps to cross the A25 (taking great care), descending steps on the far side to bear right along a field edge. In 400 yards (400m) go through a hedge gap and down to the road by the Red Lion pub.

Deep Lanes

Stop in at the excellent Red Lion (if you're not content to wait for the equally welcoming The Dolphin a few minutes along the way). Take time to notice the deep-sunk lanes around Betchworth, thick with snowdrops in late winter and primroses in spring. Centuries of hooves, boots and cartwheels have dug these high-sided holloways out of the soft local chalk and greensand.

Turn right for 100 yards (100m); left by Ye Old Gatehouse; follow fingerposts and yellow arrows for 300 yards (300m) past gardens, over a drive and down steps to a road (215502). Turn right for 300 yards (300m) to a T-junction; turn right along Wonham Lane for 400 yards (400m) to the T-junction by The Dolphin (211497 – Betchworth forge is just on your right).

Betchworth Forge

'We're a working forge, a proper forge', declares the Betchworth blacksmith, and his products prove his assertion. Since horses disappeared from the working landscape, the few country blacksmiths that still ply their trade have had to turn their hands and skills to all manner of different work. Betchworth forge turns out fancy railings, barbecues and beautifully crafted decorative ironwork for the homes and gardens of the immaculate Surrey villages nearby, but it also does all sorts of jobbing metalwork repairs and produces practical necessities such as curtain rails, brackets, firebacks, gates and handrails. If you're lucky the smith may be at work, hammering away by his furnace and occasionally plunging hot iron into water with a fizz and hiss. It's satisfying to hear that noise, and pleasing to know that the sooty old craft clings on among the shiny people-carriers and well-scrubbed lifestyles of Surrey.

Cross the road ('Greensand Way/GW' fingerpost); go through an arch and on through the churchyard.

Betchworth, Brockham, Buckland and the River Mole Valley

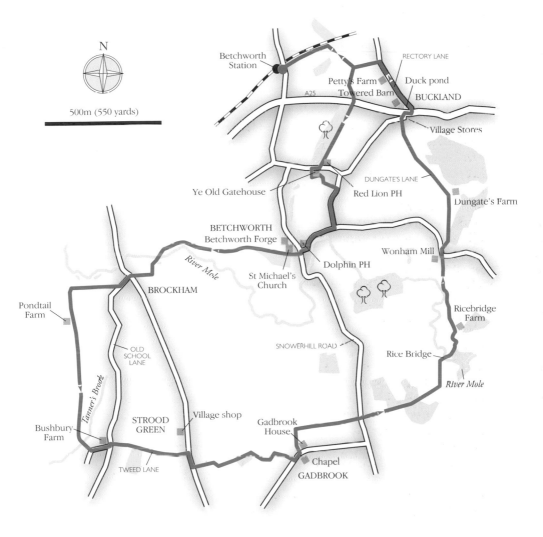

N

500m (550 yards)

Betchworth Station

RECTORY LANE

Petty's Farm
Towered Barn

Duck pond

BUCKLAND

A25

Village Stores

DUNGATE'S LANE

Ye Old Gatehouse

Red Lion PH

Dungate's Farm

BETCHWORTH
Betchworth Forge

Wonham Mill

River Mole

St Michael's
Church

Dolphin PH

BROCKHAM

Pondtail
Farm

Ricebridge
Farm

OLD
SCHOOL
LANE

SNOWERHILL ROAD

Rice Bridge

River Mole

Tanner's Brook

Bushbury
Farm

STROOD
GREEN

Village shop

Gadbrook
House

Chapel

GADBROOK

TWEED LANE

Continue along a fenced path (GW) for ³/₄ mile (1.25km) to cross the River Mole (199497). Follow GW to a road and turn right to Brockham village green.

Brockham and its Farming Countryside

Along the path through the fields the garden gates of Brockham give on to a child's wilderness paradise: tangles of scrub, swing trees, thickets and bramble-bush dens, and the grey River Mole full of moorhens. These jungly outskirts make a fine contrast to the chocolate-box perfection of the gorgeous old houses around Brockham's wide village green. Brockham might look like a set for a romantic TV fable of English village life, but out in the surrounding countryside you'll find that the local farms are far from airbrushed. Farmyards are muddy and ramshackle, the buildings as patched and pragmatic as farm buildings anywhere. Surrey farmers don't live Hollywood lives, that's for sure.

Cross the road (196495) and keep ahead down Old School Lane. In 100 yards (100m) turn right (GW) along a stony lane. In 400 yards (400m) turn left over a stile (191495 – GW, yellow arrow). Cross Pondtail Farm drive; in 50 yards (50m), GW turns right (191491), but keep ahead here for ²/₃ mile (1km), over stiles (yellow arrows), until you bear left across Tanner's Brook to walk between Bushbury Farm house and buildings (191481 – very muddy indeed!). Go through a gate into a lane (192480 – fingerpost). Turn left to cross Bushbury Lane, and follow Tweed Lane to cross the road in Strood Green (201480). NB – the village shop is just along the road to the left.

Strood Green and the Shop that Didn't Die

Strood Green is one of the very many English villages whose most basic amenities have come under threat from the inexorable rise of car ownership and of Internet and supermarket shopping. But this is a community that fought back. They have revitalised their village shop by their own efforts, and it now offers all kinds of home-made and locally produced food, as well as fulfilling the roles of a café with internet and postal facilities and a book exchange. It's a vibrant hub of community life full of news, views and lots of gossip. It's exemplary. If you want something doing properly ...

Opposite above: The Towered Barn overlooks Buckland village green and duckpond. Opposite below: The handsome old pump house still shelters the village well on Brockham's wide green.

Turn right for 150 yards (150m); then turn left (fingerpost) into the fields, following along the hedges (stiles, fingerposts, yellow arrows) for ⅓ mile (0.5km). Skirt to the right of a house (stile, yellow arrow) to meet a drive (208479 – four-finger post). Turn right here to Gadbrook Road (209477). Bear left for 200 yards (200m); opposite Gadbrook Chapel, turn left past Gadbrook House (fingerpost). In 150 yards (150m), bear right (210481) across a field for ⅓ mile (0.5km) to cross Snowerhill Road (216482 – fingerpost). Continue through Knight's Gorse wood; follow the path (fingerpost) across a field and down to cross the River Mole over Rice Bridge (223487). In 50 yards (50m), ignore a stile and yellow arrow on your right; instead, keep ahead along a sunken lane.

Pillbox and Flowers

This is a beautiful old lane, always flowery in spring and summer; a shady and sheltered old thoroughfare through the fields. Strange to think that Second World War military planners envisaged it being on the front line in the event of a German invasion. This explains the presence of the crumbling old pillbox, or strongpoint, sited here to command the crossing of the River Mole if the enemy should choose this route to advance on London.

Approaching Ricebridge Farm, turn left over a stile (224488) to bear right around the farmhouse; then steer ahead for ⅓ mile (0.5km) to disused Wonham Mill (224496). Turn left along the road for 50 yards (50m), then right (fingerpost), and immediately left again over a stile past the old millpond. Cross paddocks (stiles, gates) for ¼ mile (0.4km) to Dungate's Farm drive (224501). Turn left up Dungates Lane and follow it for ½ mile (0.75km) to cross the A25 in Buckland (221508; please take care!).

Buckland

It's certainly worth taking an hour to explore Buckland, one of the most attractive villages in the area with its three village greens, lovely old houses and curious little wind-powered sawmill. The big duck pond on the green that you cross is overlooked by the weatherboarded Towered Barn, nearly 400 years old, whose tower (according to local stories) once held tanks that supplied the whole village with water pumped up from below.

Make sure you visit Buckland Deli & Gifts, the village stores, just at the top of Dungates Lane before you cross the A25. It has a wide variety of baked goods and some very strange (in a good way) thirst-quenching drinks!

Go up Rectory Lane past the village duck pond. Continue along the lane for ¼ mile (0.4km) to pass Petty's Farm (220511). In another 100 yards (100m) turn left (FP fingerpost) past a cottage, through a kissing gate, and follow the hedge on your right. Continue through the hedge gap (217513), and aim up the next field to the left of a house, to go through a kissing gate beside the railway (215515). Turn left along the edge of the railway cutting to reach Betchworth Station.

23. LISS, SELBORNE & THE HANGERS WAY

This long day's walk in Hampshire's glorious countryside takes you to Selborne, an enchanting village forever associated with its 18th-century curate, Gilbert White, whose *Natural History and Antiquities of Selborne* became one of the best-selling books ever written. You can visit White's house, The Wakes, which also contains an exhibition devoted to Lawrence Oates, Antarctic explorer and self-sacrificial hero. Other delights of the walk include two fascinating village churches, gorgeous (if muddy) bridlepaths through the beech woods, and old-fashioned sunken lanes that are a real pleasure to ramble in.

START AND FINISH:	Liss Station
LENGTH OF WALK:	15 miles (24km)
OS MAPS:	1:50,000 Landranger 186; 1:25,000 Explorer 133
TRAVEL:	By rail from London Waterloo (1 hr 5 mins); by road – M25 (Jct 10), A3.
FEATURES:	Sunken lanes and beech woods; Church of the Holy Rood, Empshott; Gilbert White's House and Garden and The Oates Collection at Selborne; Gilbert White's grave and other White-related sites around Selborne; the Zig-Zag and the Hanger; Selborne Common; Holtham Lane and Button's Lane; Church of St Peter and St Paul, Hawkley.
REFRESHMENTS:	Queen's at Selborne and Selborne Arms, Selborne; Hawkley Inn, Hawkley.

Opposite: As these two landscapes show, little has changed in a walker's view of Gilbert White's Hampshire since the curate of Selborne wandered his local countryside.

From Liss Station (777277), cross the railway level crossing and walk up the village street. Turn left into the churchyard, and go through the gap in the hedge on the north side of the church (775279). Continue along the right side of the field and through a kissing gate to cross a road. Carry on along a green lane to cross another road (771284); up steps and on. In 100 yards (100m) turn left over a stile (yellow arrow) and continue ahead to skirt the graveyard of West Liss church. Go through a gate in the corner of the field (FP fingerpost) and cross the A3 dual carriageway by a bridge. Go through the gate on the far side and keep ahead (FP fingerpost and yellow arrow). In 150 yards (150m) cross a stile, and cross the field ahead, aiming slightly left to a stile by a gate (764286). Cross, and go along the field edge (fenced farm track) with the hedge on your left. Opposite Berrygrove Farm cross a stile, and continue to cross two more stiles. In 200 yards (200m) turn right (758288), and follow the fenced path round to the left over a stile (FP fingerpost). In 100 yards (100m) cross another stile (758288), and follow the fenced path round to the left over a stile (FP fingerpost). In 100 yards (100m) cross another stile (757289) and turn left along a wide green lane.

In 200 yards (200m) turn right through a gate (756289; FP fingerpost, 'Scotland Farm' sign; NB – homeward route (see page 176) rejoins here) and up a fenced path on the left edge of a field to reach the exit gate just before Scotland Farm's yard.

Don't go through, but instead go left over a stile (755291 – FP fingerpost). Walk up through the next field, following the hedge to your right to exit at a road. Turn left and walk steeply uphill, following the road as it meanders through a belt of trees. Pass Uplands, then at the following left bend turn right (750295 – BW fingerpost) through a gate. Follow the bridleway round the right edge of a field; in 300 yards (300m) bear right (BW fingerpost) down tree-root 'steps' to turn right along a sunken lane. In 100 yards (100m) the lane forks by Mabbotts house; don't take the right fork, but keep ahead on the level along Standfast Lane.

Sunken Lanes

The sunken lanes of east Hampshire are beautiful, if extremely muddy, and Standfast Lane is no exception. The hooves and feet of the centuries have worn a deep channel in the soft clay and chalk of the fields. The banks are mossy and well grown with field maple and hazel interspersed with large ash and beech trees. In spring there are drifts of violets and primroses in the hedge roots, and there always seems to be a light trickle of birdsong flowing from the woods.

After $1/3$ mile (0.5km) go through a gate; in another 125 yards (125m) turn left over a stile (755305 – FP fingerpost) along a ride running west between two woodlands. In 200 yards (200m) cross a stile, and keep ahead with a wood close on your left. Cross two more stiles; then, within sight of a

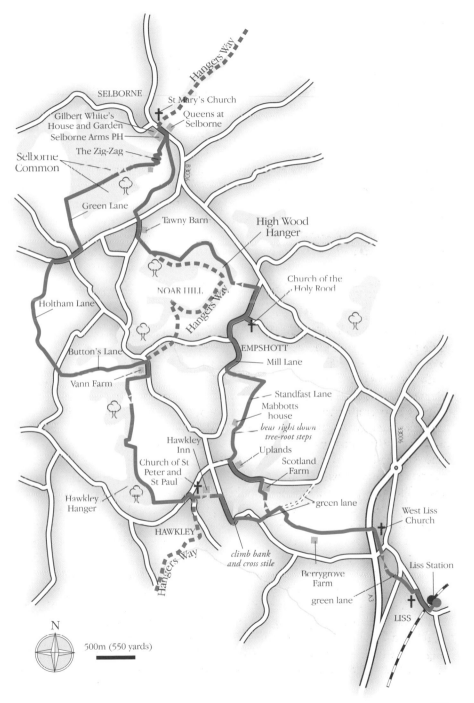

SELBORNE

St Mary's Church

Gilbert White's House and Garden
Selborne Arms PH
The Zig-Zag

Queens at Selborne

Hangers Way

Selborne Common

Green Lane

Tawny Barn

High Wood Hanger

B3006

NOAR HILL

Church of the Holy Rood

Hangers Way

Holtham Lane

EMPSHOTT

Button's Lane

Mill Lane

Vann Farm

Standfast Lane

Mabbotts house
bear right down tree-root steps

Hawkley Inn

Uplands

Church of St Peter and St Paul

Scotland Farm

green lane

B3006

Hawkley Hanger

West Liss Church

HAWKLEY

Hangers Way

climb bank and cross stile

Berrygrove Farm

Liss Station

green lane

A3

LISS

N

500m (550 yards)

house, bear right (yellow arrows) over a stile and along a stretch of fenced path to cross a stream. Climb the bank to cross a stile into Mill Lane (750307 – FP fingerpost). Turn right to walk into Empshott, ignoring the sign for Empshott Green. As you enter the village, turn right to reach the Church of the Holy Rood (753313).

Church of the Holy Rood, Empshott

Holy Rood is a lovely early 13th-century church, set on a knoll looking out over woods. It is full of curiosities and delights – side aisles so narrow that you can hardly squeeze between the nave arcade and the outer walls; ornate Victorian woodwork up in the roof; two fine William Kemp windows (St Michael with large green wings and St George looking as pretty as a young girl in a fur-trimmed cloak); solid, plain medieval pews and Jacobean altar rails.

From the church, return to the road junction and turn right for ¼ mile (0.4km). Fifty yards (50m) before a T-junction with the B3006, turn left through a gate (754317 – bridleway fingerpost) down a field edge, over a fence and up a field slope to cross a stile and turn right inside High Wood Hanger (751317 – FP fingerpost). Follow the path for 1 mile (1.6km) along the lower edge of the wood. (NB – shortly after you enter the Hanger you come to a dip where the path becomes a little scrambled. Don't worry; keep walking to your right to leave the dip and the path soon becomes clear again.) After 1 mile (1.6km), emerge from the trees

and bear right (740321 – Hangers Way/HW green arrow waymark) along a chalky trackway to reach a road. Turn right to pass 'Tawny Barn' (named 'Lower Noar Hill Farm' on the Explorer map) and reach a T-junction (739325). Cross a stile (FP fingerpost and HW arrows) and follow the markers ahead, then right, around two sides of a field (ignoring all markers that point up the hill) and on through squeeze stiles for ¾ mile (1.25km) along field edges and then a fenced path. Continue along a lane to meet the B3006 by the Selborne Arms in Selborne (742335). Turn left for the Queen's at Selborne, Gilbert White's House and St Mary's Church.

Gilbert White and Selborne

Gilbert White (1720–1793), curate of Selborne, possessed a pair of sharp eyes and an open, enquiring mind. Everything was grist to his intellectual mill, from the orgasms of swifts to the submersible breathing apparatus of deer. He was among the first to infer the annual migration of swallows. White was operating on the cusp between the Age of Reason and the Age of Romance, and memorably blended tender emotion and precise scientific observation in his writings on the natural world as it went about its affairs around Selborne. The volume containing his letters to correspondents Daines Barrington and Thomas Pennant, published in 1788 as *The Natural History and Antiquities of Selborne*, has sold countless millions of copies and drawn innumerable admirers all over the world under the spell of the obscure country curate and his few miles of Hampshire.

The Wakes

White's lifelong home, The Wakes, is now a very well-run museum. The garden, with the ha-ha that White built, contains many of the plants that the curate enthused over and cared for. When The Wakes was up for sale in the 1950s it proved too expensive for Gilbert White devotees to buy; but the purchaser, Robert Washington Oates, allowed the house to function as a Gilbert White museum on condition that his own ancestor, Captain Lawrence Oates of the Antarctic, should also be honoured with a permanent exhibition. So there is an incongruous but fascinating Oates section, commemorating the bravery of the explorer who hauled his frostbitten, gangrenous body out of the Scott expedition tent on 17 March 1912, going into the blizzard to die alone with the immortally heroic words: 'I am just going outside. I may be some time.'

St Mary's Church, Selborne

Across the road you'll find St Mary's Church. Gilbert White's grave is discreetly indicated in the graveyard, north of the chancel. Inside St Mary's are two beautiful stained-glass windows in memory of the curate – one showing St Francis feeding a splendid collection of birds, and the other featuring three roundels with rather anthropomorphised creatures.

From St Mary's Church, return up the village street to the Queen's at Selborne and turn right, following a track (National Trust 'Selborne Common Footpath Only' sign) along the left side of the car park. The track leads up to the trees ahead at the foot of the Zig-Zag.

The Zig-Zag and Selborne Common

Climb the Zig-Zag, a back-and-forth path that rises 270 feet (80m) up the face of Selborne Hanger. The 28 zigs and zags were cut by Gilbert White and his brother in 1753. From the seat at the top (741332) there's a splendid view over Selborne. Pass the seat and turn right, with a hedge and house on your left. Continue westward on this broad path into the trees and across Selborne Common. The Common, one of Gilbert White's favourite places, is a superb open area of beech wood, oak and bracken administered by the National Trust – almost 250 acres (110ha) of tangly wild land.

The path runs for 3/4 mile (1.25km) across Selborne Common. After just over 1/2 mile (1km) it forks; take the left-hand path past an upright but sawn-off tree trunk. In 300 yards (300m) you reach the western edge of the common (729328). Turn left (BW fingerpost), and in 10 yards (10m) keep ahead (four-fingered bridleway post). Cross over this junction; continue ahead along the track with the map name of Green Lane until it reaches a road (731322). Turn right; in 150 yards (150m) go over a crossroads; in another 150 yards (150m) bear left (728320) along a green lane.

Holtham Lane and Button's Lane

This is another really fine green lane, metamorphosing from Holtham Lane into Button's Lane as it curves in a C-shape through the uplands. It is hedged by gnarled pollarded oaks, field maples and beeches, interspersed with thick blocks of holly. Leaves carpet it in parts; other stretches are stony, boggy or grassy. As Button's Lane descends towards Vann Farm, the deep channel gouged down the centre tells of its annual winter transformation into a torrent.

You follow this lane for 1³/₄ miles (3.25km). After 1 mile (1.6km) it crosses a road (728306) and swaps its name from Holtham Lane to Button's Lane. It becomes paved for a stretch, veers downhill after Keyham Farm and continues as an unpaved track again until it meets a road (739307). Turn right to pass Vann Farm and its duck pond; then turn right over a stile (Hangers Way/HW fingerpost), up a field edge with a hedge on your right. Cross a stile (HW) and continue along the field edge, bearing left at the top (737306 – FP fingerpost and HW) and following HW signs with a hedge on your right. At the far end of the field cross a stile (HW); descend steps to cross a footbridge, then ascend to bridleway fingerposts. Keep ahead (HW) on a track along the bottom edge of Hawkley Hanger for almost 1 mile (1.6km), following the HW signs, until the track leaves the wood (740290 – BW fingerpost and HW) and bears left down a field to the road in Hawkley village (745290). Turn left to the church.

Church of St Peter and St Paul, Hawkley

Hawkley's Church of St Peter and St Paul was completely rebuilt in 1865, but is an excellent example of how the Victorians sometimes got their country churches right. There are chunky, cylindrical columns in the nave arcades, their capitals richly carved. Floral corbels support the nave roof and angels embellish the aisles. Later generations have had their influence, too. The south chapel is beautified by a marvellous late 20th-century mural of local flowers, birds and animals by Sally Maltby, illuminating the theme: 'I will lift up mine eyes unto the hills'.

From the church, bear left up the road past the Hawkley Inn to a T-junction (749299). Turn right here ('West Liss 1¹/₂' sign) along the road. Go round a sharp left-hand hairpin bend, and in 40 yards (40m) climb the bank on your right and cross a stile (751287 – FP fingerpost). Aim for the bottom left corner of the field to cross a stile into a road (755288). Turn right, and immediately left along a green lane. This will return you to the gate at OS grid reference 756289 (see outward journey, page 172). Keep ahead along the green lane for 200 yards (200m) to turn right over the stile, and retrace your steps past Berrygrove Farm to Liss.

24. OVERTON, HANNINGTON & WATERSHIP DOWN

A tremendous roof-of-the-world walk that lasts all day and will leave you tired but happy, with a mind full of gorgeous downland scenes. You start in the lovely valley of the River Test amid the tree-hung reservoirs of long-defunct paper mills. A long stretch of old chalk-and-flint trackways brings you north to Hannington and its pretty church and village green, then on to the dramatic north-facing escarpment of Watership Down. Thoughts around here are of Bigwig, Fiver, Hazel and the other rabbits, whose adventures in Richard Adams's classic tale *Watership Down* were set on these uplands. Long tracks across the downs bring you south again, crossing an old Roman road running forgotten in a strip of woodland, to reach the oldest road in Britain and more scenes from *Watership Down*. From here you descend into the valley of the Test to end your long walk in lowland surroundings once more.

START AND FINISH:	Overton Station
LENGTH OF WALK:	15 miles (24km)
OS MAPS:	1:50,000 Landranger 185; 1:25,000 Explorer 144
TRAVEL:	By rail from London Waterloo (1 hr); by road – M3 (Jct 8), A303 and minor roads to Overton.
FEATURES:	Mill pools at Overton; barn at Manor Farm, North Oakley; etched windows by Laurence Whistler in All Saints Church, Hannington; Watership Down scenes; downland views and tracks; Portway Roman road in Caesar's Belt; Harrow Way ancient trackway.
REFRESHMENTS:	The Vine at Hannington.

Overton was founded by Bishop Lucy of Winchester in 1217 to provide His Grace with cash from rents. The Hampshire town beside the River Test became the site of a great sheep fair; up to 50,000 animals would be driven to the pastures by the river to be sold. Milling was big business, too – flour milling at first, then silk production and, finally, paper for bank notes. The legacy left by the mills is a long run of ponds, which snake from near the source of the river on down the valley. They make a picturesque accompaniment to the start of the walk.

From Overton Station (Platform 2; 518508) walk straight ahead down Station Approach with houses on your right. Keep ahead at a junction, and in 80 yards (80m) turn left (519504 – 'Polhampton' sign). In ¼ mile (0.4km), where the road bends right to cross the River Test (523505), take the left fork. In another ¼ mile (0.4km), beside a cottage with five dormer windows on your left (526507), bear left up a green lane, under the railway and on to a road (526512). Turn right along this quiet country lane for ¾ mile (1.25km), crossing a lane (532515) to reach a T-junction near Ashe Warren Farm (536520). A byway fingerpost points on along a green lane for another mile (1.6km).

Country Lanes of the Hampshire Downs

These country lanes of the Hampshire downs – both the tarmac motor roads and the green lanes – are remarkably quiet. You can walk for hours and see only a handful of cars on the tarred lanes, while other walkers are a rarity. This is country-lane rambling as it used to be before rural roads got crowded and drivers forgot how to go slowly and patiently.

Just before reaching cottages on White Lane, the 'Wayfarers Walk' (WW) trail crosses the green road. Turn left here through a kissing gate (551526 – FP fingerpost and WW post) along a path, bearing left in 100 yards (100m) in the outer skirt of a hazel wood. Follow WW arrows along a clear track for 1 mile (1.6km) to Freemantle Farm. Bear left through the farmyard (543537 – FP fingerpost and WW), and in 300 yards (300m) turn right (FP fingerpost and WW arrows) through a hedge and diagonally left across a field, aiming for the thatched barn at the Manor Farm, North Oakley (538541).

Manor Farm Barn

This is a lovely old building, a Tudor barn with a really fine hammerbeam roof that would grace any country church. And the barn, being still in full use, has the dignity of employment to add to the patina of centuries and the rugged strength and beauty of its construction. North Oakley is a tiny hamlet caught in a fold of the downs among large open fields of pale flinty soil, good clumps of woodland and patches of grass where hares lollop.

Turn right along the road, rounding a left bend to walk up to the hilltop village of Hannington. The Vine at Hannington (540553) is a fine pub on the southern edge of the village;

Opposite: Beech hangers ride the edge of the Watership Down escarpment under enormous billowing skies – heavenly countryside for rabbits and ramblers alike.

beyond it lies the village green, where the head of the village well is still protected by a miniature tiled broach spire that was installed to commemorate Queen Victoria's 1897 Diamond Jubilee. Beyond the well stands All Saints Church (539555).

All Saints Church, Hannington

This little crooked flint church raises its broach spire among limes and yews; a plain village church, rather barn-like, with a blocked north door and a large weather-beaten Mass dial. The church is graced by two extremely beautiful windows by Laurence Whistler (1912–2000), the celebrated glass engraver. One shows a sheaf of corn, a flock of sheep on the downs with a sheepdog intently watching them, a sunburst lighting up the scene and a shadowy scythe; it is inscribed 'Remember William Whistler, farmer, 1886–1978'. The other window, to Rose Hodson, shows a crucifix rising above a house. Rose tendrils climb from a chimney and a window to wrap themselves round the Cross and change it into a Tree of Life. 'Lord who shall dwell in thy tabernacle, or who shall rest upon thy holy hills?' asks the inscription. 'What if Earth be but the shadow of Heaven and things therein, each to other like?'

Turn left at the end of the green; the path passes down the right side of the church and doglegs right ('Footpath only' sign) round a barn. In 20 yards (20m) ignore a stile and FP fingerpost on your right (537555) and keep ahead

with a hedge on your left to go through a wicket gate. Follow the field edge, on a path between hedges, to the top of For Down (531553), then on towards Walkeridge Farm. Turn right (WW) along the hedge for 300 yards (300m) to cross a road. WW (large post) continues ahead as a green lane, soon passing under power lines. At a field edge (blue cycle route sign) cross the field where the obvious route is and continue for $^3/_4$ mile (1.25km) to cross the B3051 at the crest of White Hill (516565).

Continue along WW for $1^1/_4$ miles (2km) until you arrive opposite the northern end of Cannon Avenue beech hanger (499569) on Watership Down.

Scenes from *Watership Down*

Richard Adams, author of the celebrated novel *Watership Down* (1972), grew up hereabouts and knew this beautiful grassy down well. To amuse his daughters on long car drives he began to spin them yarns about a group of rabbits that lived in a burrow on Watership Down. The tale grew to become a full-length novel, meticulously observed, beautifully written, humorously told and immensely exciting. It was greeted coolly on first publication, but when the American public 'discovered' it two years later, *Watership Down* became a worldwide best-seller.

You can identify several of the story's locations from the crest of Watership Down. Cannon Avenue wood is the beech hanger at whose northern edge the rabbits dug their

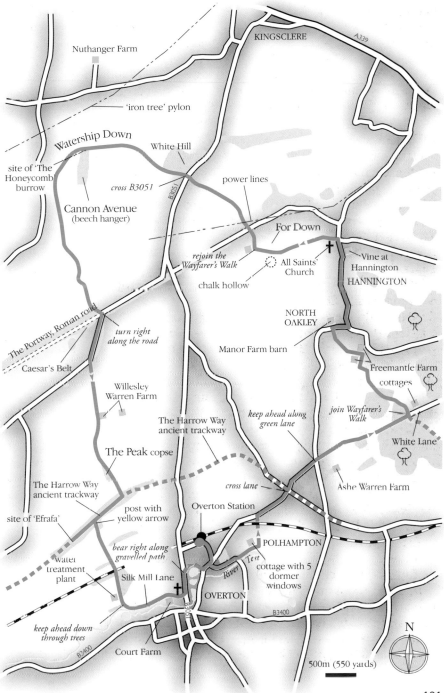

Nuthanger Farm

KINGSCLERE

A339

'iron tree' pylon

Watership Down

White Hill

site of 'The
Honeycomb
burrow

cross B3051

B3051

power lines

Cannon Avenue
(beech hanger)

For Down

*rejoin the
Wayfarer's Walk*

All Saints'
Church

Vine at
Hannington

HANNINGTON

chalk hollow

The Portway, Roman road

*turn right
along the road*

NORTH
OAKLEY

Manor Farm barn

Freemantle Farm
cottages

Caesar's Belt

Willesley
Warren Farm

*keep ahead along
green lane*

*join Wayfarer's
Walk*

White Lane

The Harrow Way
ancient trackway

The Peak copse

The Harrow Way
ancient trackway

cross lane

Ashe Warren Farm

site of 'Efrafa'

post with
yellow arrow

Overton Station

*bear right along
gravelled path*

POLHAMPTON

water
treatment
plant

River Test

cottage with 5
dormer
windows

Silk Mill Lane

OVERTON

B3051

B3400

*keep ahead down
through trees*

B3400

Court Farm

500m (550 yards)

N

181

'Honeycomb' burrow. Walk to the rim of the escarpment, which falls away 260 feet (80m) in a sudden swoop. Up this slope the rabbits toiled on their arrival after a dangerous journey from Sandleford Warren. Later in the book, Blackberry and Dandelion lured the dog from Nuthanger Farm up the escarpment to burst upon the fearsome rabbit villain General Woundwort as he was about to destroy the warren. Nuthanger Farm itself is hidden by a rise of ground below in the valley, but between the farm and the down you can see the 'iron tree' or pylon that features in the tale.

Follow the white railings of racehorse gallops on from Cannon Avenue. Soon they diverge to the right (497568); keep a hedge on your left and follow it round to the left to go through a gate ('Hants County Council Off Road Cycle Trail' arrow). Continue southwards along this track by the hedge for nearly 1½ miles (2.5km) until it bisects the long, narrow windbreak wood called Caesar's Belt and reaches a road (502543).

Caesar's Belt and the Portway Roman Road

Caesar's Belt is a 3-mile (5-km) strip of larch, hazel and beech trees. It conceals the raised causeway of the Portway, a Roman road that ran between the settlement at Old Sarum, just north of present-day Salisbury, and the town of Calleva Atrebatum or Silchester (see pages 186–9). The Portway may have existed as a route for a thousand years before the Romans came to Britain; it is thought that they simply straightened and improved what was already there.

Turn right along the road for ⅓ mile (0.5km), taking great care. At the right bend bear left on Willesley Warren farm track (500536). In just over ½ mile (0.75km) you pass Willesley Warren Farm entrance (501527). The track then becomes a green lane, which passes The Peak copse in another ½ mile (0.75km). At 350 yards (350m) beyond the copse, you reach a byway post at a junction of tracks (505515). Turn right here along the Harrow Way.

The Harrow Way

The Harrow Way can claim to be Britain's oldest road, a trackway whose course can be traced across the whole of southern England in a magnificent 250-mile (420-km) arc from Dorset to the Kentish coast. Tin-traders, farmers, hunters, drovers, warriors and pilgrims have trodden out its course over perhaps five millennia – maybe much longer. Its eastern half is now the very popular North Downs Way National Trail/Pilgrims' Way (see pages 147–62), but here along its western course it is little frequented. It runs 20 yards (20m) wide, carpeted with leaves, flanked by many tree and bush species – sycamore, oak, ash, beech, elder, hazel, yew, larch, cherry, blackthorn, whitethorn, to name but half. The Harrow Way reeks of history and human activity over the centuries – a noble high thoroughfare across the downs, cloaked in the anonymity of its dense hedges.

Follow the Harrow Way for ¹/₃ mile (0.5km), to pass a post with a yellow arrow pointing left (501511). Continue for ¹/₄ mile (0.4km) to reach a crossing of tracks at a BW fingerpost (498508).

'Efrafa'

Here Richard Adams sited 'Efrafa', the enemy warren run with military precision and brutal efficiency by that 'crack-brained slave-driver' Woundwort, as Bigwig styled him. It was here that the Watership Down rabbits came on their hazardous doe-stealing expedition, only just escaping with their lives – and with the females – in one of the tensest episodes in *Watership Down*.

From Efrafa return to the post with the yellow arrow (501511). Bear right to leave the Harrow Way and walk down through a tunnel of trees for ¹/₂ mile (0.75km) to cross the railway (504503 – please take care!) by steep steps. Continue past a water treatment plant and on down a lane for 200 yards (200m). Where it bends right (505498 – yellow arrow on a post) keep ahead down through trees (ignoring Southington Lane, which forks to the right), to bear left along Silk Mill Lane for ¹/₃ mile (0.5km). Turn right at a junction (512499), and in 150 yards (150m) bear left along Church Road to meet the B3051 (515499). Cross the road and turn left along the pavement; then in 300 yards (300m) bear right (515502 – FP fingerpost) along a gravelled path round a mill reservoir to meet a road (518503). Turn left to reach Overton Station.

25. STRATFIELD MORTIMER, SILCHESTER ROMAN TOWN & THE DEVIL'S HIGHWAY

This walk follows some fascinating ancient trackways on the Berkshire/Hampshire border, including a stretch of the old Roman road long known as the Devil's Highway. You'll walk the Roman walls that encircle the Romano-British city of Calleva Atrebatum, today called Silchester. Lovers of stained glass can admire some beautiful pieces in St Mary's Church at Stratfield Mortimer, while the other St Mary's on the route – built right on Silchester's Roman walls – boasts fine craftsmanship covering 700 years.

START AND FINISH:	Mortimer Station
LENGTH OF WALK:	9 miles (14km)
OS MAPS:	1:50,000 Landranger 175; 1:25,000 Explorer 159
TRAVEL:	By rail from London Paddington (50 mins approx.); by road – M4 (Jct 11), A33, minor roads west from B3349 at Riseley.
FEATURES:	Saxon grave slab and medieval glass in St Mary's Church, Stratfield Mortimer; 13th-century stonework, 15th-century angel screen, medieval tombs and wall painting in St Mary's Church, Silchester; Roman amphitheatre and the Roman town of Calleva Atrebatum at Silchester; the Devil's Highway.
REFRESHMENTS:	Cinnamon Tree Indian restaurant, Stratfield Mortimer.

From Platform 2 at Stratfield Mortimer station (672641), leave the station, walk up to the road and turn left. In 100 yards (100m) turn left at the mini-roundabout, pass the Cinnamon Tree restaurant, and in 250 yards (250m) turn left (669642 – BW fingerpost) to St Mary's Church.

St Mary's Church, Stratfield Mortimer

St Mary's has to be kept locked; but it is well worth arranging a visit (see page 200) and adding the extra half-hour to your walk in order to see its two ancient treasures.

The Saxon grave slab fixed to the south wall of the chancel is inscribed: 'On the eight before the Kalends of October [24 September], Aegelward son of Kypping was laid in this place. Blessed be the man who prays for his soul. Toki made me.' Toki was the name of one of King Canute's courtiers, which would date this grave slab to about AD 1000.

Go through the little door between the grave slab and the organ to find St Mary's ancient stained glass gathered in a three-light lancet window cramped behind the organ. These are beautiful fragments. In the central lancet, William of Wykeham, founder of Winchester College, takes centre stage with a many-folded face and his motto 'Manners Maketh Man' inscribed beside him. In the right-hand panel we see Christ labelled 'Salvator Mundi' (Saviour of the World) with a sunburst behind him and a globe in his hand; above him the prodigal son sits despondently under a tree in a farmyard where a herd of pigs is enthusiastically gobbling swill. The left panel is a fine naturalistic scene labelled 'November', showing two yeomen cutting down leafless trees while a centaur in the middle distance aims his bow.

Leaving the church door, turn right through the churchyard. Cross a footbridge, keep a pond on your right and follow the field edge. In 1/4 mile (0.4km) bear right over a footbridge (666637 – FP fingerpost), then turn left with the stream on your left. In 250 yards (250m) ignore a plank footbridge on your left; in another 300 yards (300m) turn left over a stile (664634) and continue in the same direction as before, keeping the stream on your left. At the far end of the field cross a stile (yellow arrow) and follow the left-hand field edge round to the right to cross a stile and reach a road (657632). Turn left. In 400 yards (400m), at a T-junction, bear left past Brocas Lands Farm; at the next left bend keep ahead (653630) along a green lane. In 250 yards (250m) ignore the FP fingerpost on your right to follow the lane for 3/4 mile (1.25km) to a road.

Green Lane

This old green lane is one of those sunken, secret ways through the fields that wind across so much of England's landscape. Walking its rutted channel gives a sense of connection with a distant agricultural past. Bulbous oaks and field maples line its hedges. It is extremely muddy in parts, and prone to landslips; the sandy, gravelly soil is liable to burst out of the banks and half-block the way.

The green lane follows its own logic as to twists and turns; logic obscured nowadays, since the fields and farms it served have shifted their relationships with each other, and their levels of accessibility and importance, since this modest trackway's heyday as a vital local communication route.

At the road (645625), keep ahead for 200 yards (250m) past Manor Farm to find St Mary's Church, Silchester, on your right (643624).

St Mary's Church, Silchester

St Mary's stands right on the Roman wall that encloses the 100-acre (40-ha) site of Calleva Atrebatum, the Romano-British city that the Saxons came to call Silchester. The wall stands 6 feet (2m) high hereabouts, its flint cobbles and stone laid in layers, herringbone style. St Mary's is a remarkable church; it was built on a site reckoned to be sacred since pagan times, and continues a tradition of Christian worship in this location dating back to a little 4th-century basilica that has been excavated amid the ruins of Calleva Atrebatum.

St Mary's 15th-century chancel screen is exceptional; it contains 15 broad-winged angels, each crouched uncomfortably on a bent left knee. It was hidden in a barn to save it from destruction during the Reformation upheavals, and restored to the church some 300 years later. The red-and-yellow floral designs painted round the chancel windows must date to when the chancel was built around 1230. But St Mary's is not just a museum of medieval art. There are plain but beautiful early 20th-century bench ends carved with biblical plants – palm, apple, olive, mulberry, bulrush, cucumber and more. And over the font hangs a modern wrought-iron corona featuring seeds – or are they crucifixion nails? – bursting into flower.

From the church, follow the path through the churchyard to the north-east corner. Two kissing gates lead to a gravelled lane, which takes you through the middle of the site of Calleva Atrebatum. At the far side, turn right through a kissing gate (636625; 'Silchester Trail' waymark) to walk a half circuit of the Roman walls back to the road beside Manor Farm.

Roman Town of Calleva Atrebatum

The walls of Calleva Atrebatum, made of flint with stone courses, were built around AD 270, and their ring of almost 2 miles (3.2km) is

Opposite: You can walk a circuit on a flinty path that runs along the top of the Roman walls at Calleva Atrebatum.

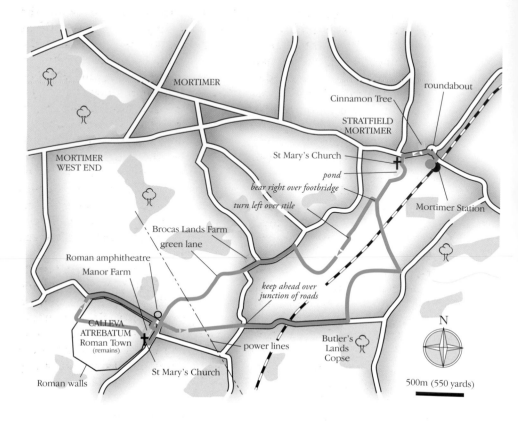

MORTIMER

roundabout

Cinnamon Tree

STRATFIELD
MORTIMER

MORTIMER
WEST END

St Mary's Church

pond

bear right over footbridge

Mortimer Station

turn left over stile

Brocas Lands Farm

green lane

Roman amphitheatre

Manor Farm

*keep ahead over
junction of roads*

CALLEVA
ATREBATUM
Roman Town
(remains)

power lines

Butler's
Lands
Copse

N

St Mary's Church

Roman walls

500m (550 yards)

reckoned the finest run of Roman wall in Britain. They were built to strengthen the earthen ramparts put up here by the Romans shortly after they conquered Britain in the 1st century AD. The Romans superimposed their town of Calleva Atrebatum, 'the place in the woods where the Atrebates dwell', on a settlement of the Atrebates tribe that had been established for at least a century. Not that the Atrebates were themselves locals; they were a Belgic tribe, a warrior aristocracy that had fled to Britain after a failed rising against the Roman occupation of Gaul. Once established here, they lorded it over the local tribes until the coming of the Romans. The Atrebates did not care for quislings; when their own king Commius brought them a message from Julius Caesar ordering them to submit to the 'protection of the Romans', they threw him in prison and loaded him with chains.

Calleva Atrebatum grew to be one of the major Roman garrison towns of southern England. The haphazardly sited Celtic houses were replaced by a regular grid of streets. Buildings were at first of timber, but were rebuilt in stone a century or so after the foundation of the Roman town. They included a colonnaded forum, baths, temples, shops, houses and a large inn with a courtyard – also the Christian church. The town had its own mint, too. Living conditions were spacious, even gracious: houses had an acre of ground to themselves. Artefacts uncovered during the early 20th-century excavation of the town include mosaics, ornamental plasterwork, wooden barrels and buckets, jewellery in bronze and gold, surgical instruments and domestic tools, knives and candlesticks.

Calleva Atrebatum seems to have flourished until the Romans left Britain around AD 410, then limped on until the invading Saxons burned it around AD 500. Some tales say that Aella the Saxon gathered sparrows and sent them into the city with firebrands tied to their tails. Others tell how King Arthur was crowned at Calleva before its destruction.

Back at the road by Manor Farm, turn left. In 100 yards (100m) go round a left bend to find Calleva's Roman amphitheatre on the right side of the road (645626).

Amphitheatre of
Calleva Atrebatum

This large, bowl-shaped open-air theatre was built between AD 50 and AD 75, at the time of the foundation of Calleva Atrebatum. As with the town's buildings, it too started life as an earth-and-timber structure before being rebuilt in stone in the 3rd century AD. The big stone-walled circle with its high, sloped banks was capable of accommodating 3,500 customers seated, or 7,000 standing: they would have watched triumphal ceremonies, theatrical spectacles and gladiatorial combat. Judging by the provenance of most of the bones unearthed, horses were the principal victims. The amphitheatre had been abandoned by the time the Romans left Britain.

From the amphitheatre, return to Manor Farm house. Directly opposite is a gap in the hedge and a footpath leading across a large field and under power lines. Follow this path, and at the far side of the field keep ahead over a road junction and along the lane.

The Devil's Highway

This very long, straight lane, known for over a thousand years as the Devil's Highway, runs for many miles under various guises: as a tarmac road, a green lane, a muddy channel through fields and a faint scoop in the floor of woods. During the Dark Ages, with the Roman occupation long forgotten, superstitious folk reckoned that only the Devil could have built and paved a road so long and straight. But in fact the Romans built it as a highway to connect Calleva Atrebatum with London, some 40 miles (64km) to the east.

Cross the railway and keep ahead, ignoring the footpath that turns left opposite Jackdaw House. About 600 yards (600m) beyond the railway you reach Butlers Lands Copse on your right. Here leave the road (663625), taking the footpath left into the field opposite the copse (FP). Follow the left side of a hedge. In 350 yards (350m) bear right (waymark arrow) across an open field to reach the end of a hedge ahead. Keep forward with the hedge on your left for 300 yards (300m), to turn left along a green lane (668631). At the lane's end keep ahead (arrow) to cross under the railway (667634). Aim diagonally right across the next field (arrow) to reach a footbridge over a ditch (666637). Don't cross, but turn right to Stratfield Mortimer.

Opposite above: Silchester's two-mile ring of Roman wall, built of flint, stone and tiles, stands 15 feet (5m) high in places and is reputed to be the finest surviving run of Roman wall in Britain.
Opposite below: The pretty 15th-century Church of St Mary, Silchester, is sited on a spot believed sacred since pagan times, and was a place of Christian worship as far back as the 4th century AD.

FURTHER INFORMATION

1. GORING & MAPLEDURHAM

Mapledurham House, Mill and Tea Room
The Estate Office, Mapledurham House, Reading, Oxfordshire, RG4 7TR
Tel: 0118 972 3350
www.mapledurham.co.uk
Opening hours: *Easter Saturday–end of September* Saturday, Sunday and Bank Holidays 2pm–5.30pm

The Swan
Shooters Hill, Pangbourne, Reading, Berkshire, RG8 7DU
Tel: 0118 984 4494
www.swanpangbourne.com
Food-serving times: every day 10am–9pm

2. HENLEY-ON-THAMES, GREYS COURT & ROTHERFIELD PEPPARD

Greys Court
Rotherfield Greys, Henley-on-Thames, Oxfordshire, RG9 4PG
Tel: 01494 755564
www.nationaltrust.org.uk
Opening hours:
House April–October: Wednesday–Saturday 11am–5pm
Gardens April–October: Tuesday–Saturday 2pm–6pm

La Ruchetta
Peppard Common, Henley-on-Thames, Oxfordshire, RG9 5JU
Tel: 01491 628343
www.ruchetta.com/peppard
Opening hours: Tuesday–Saturday 12pm–2.30pm, 6.30pm–10pm

Maltsters Arms PH
Rotherfield Greys, Henley-on-Thames, Oxfordshire, RG9 4QD
Tel: 01491 628400
www.maltsters.co.uk
Food-serving times: Monday–Saturday 12pm–2.15pm, 6.15pm–9.15pm; Sunday 12pm–2.30pm

Red Lion PH
Peppard Common, Henley-on-Thames, Oxfordshire, RG9 5LB
Tel: 01491 628329
Food-serving times: Monday–Friday 12.30pm–2.45pm, 6pm–8.45pm; Saturday 12pm–9pm; Sunday 12pm–6pm

St Nicholas's Church
Rotherfield Greys, Henley-on-Thames, Oxfordshire, RG9 4QB
www.chord.demon.co.uk/greys/

3. GREAT MISSENDEN, HUGHENDEN & HIGH WYCOMBE

Church of St Michael and All Angels
Valley Road, Hughenden Valley, High Wycombe, Buckinghamshire, HP14
www.hughendenparishchurch.org.uk
Opening hours: daily dawn–dusk

Hughenden Manor
High Wycombe, Buckinghamshire, HP14 4LA
Tel: 01494 755565
www.nationaltrust.org.uk
Opening hours: see website

Origins at the White Lion
57 High Street, Great Missenden, Buckinghamshire, HP16 0AL

Tel: 01494 863696
www.originswinebar.co.uk/
Food-serving times: Monday–Saturday
12pm–2pm and 6pm–9.30pm; Sunday
12pm–2pm

Polecat Inn
170 Wycombe Road, Prestwood, Great
Missenden, Buckinghamshire, HP16 0HJ
Tel: 01494 862253
Food-serving times: Monday–Sunday
12pm–3pm and 6pm–10pm

4. BERKHAMSTED COMMON, ASHRIDGE HOUSE & FRITHSDEN BEECHES

Ashridge House
Ashridge, Berkhamsted,
Hertfordshire, HP4 1NS
Tel: 01442 843491
www.ashridge.org.uk
Opening hours:
Grounds Saturday and Sunday 2pm–6pm;
House This is a private property with very
limited public opening hours, always check
website for details

Berkhamsted Castle
Berkhamsted, Hertfordshire, HP4 1LJ
Tel: 0870 333 1181 (English Heritage)
www.berkhamsted-castle.org.uk
Opening hours: winter 10am–4pm; summer
10am–6pm

5. LITTLE CHALFONT TO LATIMER, CHURCH END & CHENIES

Chenies Manor House and Gardens
Chenies, Buckinghamshire, WD3 6ER
Tel: 01494 762888
www.cheniesmanorhouse.co.uk
Opening times: see website

The Cock Inn
Church End, Church Lane, Sarratt

Hertfordshire, WD3 6HH
Tel: 01923 282908
www.cockinn.net
Food-serving times: Monday
12pm–2.30pm; Tuesday–Saturday
12pm–2.30pm and 6pm–9pm; Sunday
12pm–4pm

6. HARLINGTON, BUNYAN'S OAK & SHARPENHOE CLAPPERS

The Lynmore PH
Sharpenhoe Road, Sharpenhoe,
Bedford, Bedfordshire, MK45 4SH
Tel: 01582 881233
Food-serving times: Monday–Saturday
12pm–9pm; Sunday 12pm–6pm

7. WATTON-AT-STONE, BENINGTON LORDSHIP & SACOMBE

All Saints' Church
Church Lane, Little Munden, Hertfordshire,
SG12 0NR
www.achurchnearyou.com/littlemunden/
Opening hours: by arrangement with key-
holder; details posted at church

The Bell
4 Town Lane, Benington,
Hertfordshire, SG2 7LA
Tel: 01438 869270
www.thebellbenington.co.uk
Food-serving times: Monday 12pm–2pm;
Tuesday–Saturday 12pm–2pm, 7pm–9pm;
Sunday 12pm–3.30pm

Benington Lordship
Stevenage, Hertfordshire, SG2 7BS
Tel: 08701 261709
www.beningtonlordship.co.uk
Opening hours: see website

The Boot
Munden Road, Dane End, Ware,
Hertfordshire, SG12 0LH
www.the-boot-dane-end.co.uk
Tel: 01920 438770

Church of St Andrew and St Mary
Church Lane, Watton-at-Stone,
Hertfordshire, SG14 3RD
www.achurchnearyou.com/watton-at-stone
Opening hours: April–October Sunday
2.30pm–5pm

George and Dragon PH
82 High Street, Watton-at-Stone,
Hertford, Hertfordshire
Tel: 01920 830285
www.georgeanddragonwatton.co.uk/
Food-serving times: Monday–Saturday
lunch 12pm–2.30pm; Sunday lunch 12pm–
3.00pm; Sunday–Thursday evening 6pm–
9pm; Friday–Saturday evening 6pm–10pm

St Catherine's Church
Nr Sacombe Green, Sacombe,
Hertfordshire
www.achurchnearyou.com/sacombe/
Opening hours: by arrangement with key-
holder; details posted at church

St Peter's Church
Church Green, Benington,
Stevenage, Hertfordshire
www.ubbw.org.uk/
Opening hours: daily 9.30am–dusk

8. NEWPORT, WIDDINGTON & DEBDEN

Fleur-de-Lys PH
High Street, Widdington,
Essex, CB11 3SG
Tel: 01799 543280
www.thefleurdelys.co.uk
Food-serving times: no food served on
Monday; Tuesday–Saturday 12pm–2.30pm,
6.30pm–9pm; Sunday 12pm–3pm

Mole Hall Wildlife Park
Widdington, Nr Saffron Walden,
Essex, CB11 3SS
Tel: 01799 540400
www.molehall.com

Prior's Hall Barn
Widdington, Nr Newport, Essex
Tel: 0870 333 1181 (English Heritage)
www.english-heritage.org.uk
Opening hours: *April–September* Saturday
and Sunday 10am–6pm

White Horse Inn
Belmont Hill, Newport,
Saffron Walden, Essex, CB11 3RF
Tel: 01799 540002
No food served

The White Hart
High Street, Debden, Essex, CB11 3LE

9. KELVEDON, COGGESHALL & FEERING

All Saints' Church
The Street, Feering, Colchester,
Essex, CO5 9QJ
www.achurchnearyou.com/feering-all-
saints/

Bell Inn
The Street, Feering, Colchester,
Essex, CO5 9QQ
Tel: 01376 570375
Food-serving times: Monday–Saturday
12pm–2pm; Tuesday–Saturday
6.30pm–9pm; Sunday 12.30pm–2pm

The Chapel Inn
4 Market Hill, Coggeshall, Colchester,
Essex, CO6 1TS
Tel: 01376 561655
www.thechapelinn.com
Food-serving times: no food served
Tuesday; lunch Monday, Wednesday–
Saturday 12pm–2pm; lunch Sunday

12pm–3pm; evenings Thursday–Saturday
7pm–9pm

Church of St Peter-ad-Vincula
Church Street, Coggeshall,
Colchester, Essex
www.st-peter-ad-vincula.org.uk

Coggeshall Grange Barn
Grange Hill, Coggeshall,
Colchester, Essex, CO6 1RE
Tel: 01376 562226
www.nationaltrust.org.uk
Opening hours: *April–October* Wednesday–
Sunday 1pm–5pm

Paycocke's
25 West Street, Coggeshall,
Colchester, Essex, CO6 1NS
Tel: 01376 561305
www.nationaltrust.org.uk
Opening hours: *March–April* Saturday and
Sunday 1pm–5pm; *April–October*
Wednesday–Sunday 11am–5pm

The Woolpack
91 Church Street, Coggeshall, Colchester,
Essex, CO6 1UB
Tel: 01376 561235

10. INGATESTONE, BUTTSBURY & MOUNTNESSING HALL

Church of St Giles Mountnessing
Church Road, Mountnessing, Essex
Tel: see website
www.stgilesmountnessing.co.uk
Opening hours: see website

Ingatestone Hall
Hall Lane, Ingatestone, Essex, CM4 9NR
Tel: 01277 353010
www.ingatestonehall.com
Opening hours: *Easter–September*
Wednesday (except in June), Sunday and
Bank Holidays 12pm–5pm

11. ROCHFORD & PAGLESHAM

Cherry Tree PH
Stambridge Road, Rochford,
Essex, SS4 2AF
Tel: 01702 544426
www.thecherrytree-rochford.co.uk
Food-serving times: Monday–Friday
12pm–2pm, 7pm–9.30pm; Sunday
12pm–8pm

Plough and Sail PH
East End, Paglesham, nr Rochford,
Essex, SS4 2EQ
Tel: 01702 258242
www.theploughandsail.co.uk
Food-serving times: daily 12pm–2pm,
7pm–9.30pm

Punch Bowl PH
Paglesham Churchend, Rochford,
Essex, SS4 2DP
Tel: 01702 258376
Food-serving times: Monday–Saturday
12pm–3pm, 6.30pm–9pm; Sunday
12pm–8pm

St Andrew's Church
Hall Road, Rochford, Essex, SS4 1NL
www.achurchnearyou.com/rochford-st-
andrew

12. SHOREHAM, LULLINGSTONE & EYNSFORD

Eynsford Castle
Eynsford, Kent, DA4 0AA
Tel: 0870 333 1181 (English Heritage)
www.english-heritage.org.uk
Opening hours: see website

Lullingstone Castle
Eynsford, Kent, DA4 0JA
Tel: 01322 862114
www.lullingstonecastle.co.uk
Opening hours: see website

Lullingstone Roman Villa
Lullingstone Lane, Eynsford, Kent, DA4 0JA
Tel: 0870 333 1181 (English Heritage)
www.english-heritage.org.uk
Opening hours: *April–September* daily
10am–6pm; *October* daily 10am–4pm;
November–March daily 10am–4pm

St Botolph's Church
Lullingstone, Sevenoaks, Kent
Tel: see website
www.efl-churches.org/friends_stbot.htm
Opening hours: see website

Ye Olde George Inn
Church Street, Shoreham,
Sevenoaks, Kent, TN14 7RY
Tel: 01959 522017
Food-serving times: daily 12pm–3pm,
6pm–9pm

13. TEYNHAM, CONYER & THE SWALE

Castle Inn
2 The Street, Oare, Faversham,
Kent, ME13 0PY
Tel: 01795 533674
Food-serving times: Monday–Saturday
12pm–2.20pm; Sunday 12pm–3pm

St Mary's Church
Teynham, Kent
Tel: 01795 522510 (rectory)/521538
(church warden)
www.faversham.org/pages/standard.aspx?i_
PageID=11107
Opening hours: see website

Ship Inn
The Quay, Conyer, Sittingbourne,
Kent, ME9 9HR
Tel: 01795 520881
www.shipinnconyer.co.uk
Food-serving times: daily lunchtimes
and evenings

Three Mariners PH
2 Church Road, Oare, Faversham,
Kent, ME13 0QA
Tel: 01795 533633
www.thethreemarinersoare.co.uk
Food-serving times: Monday–Saturday
12pm–2.30pm (Saturday till 3pm),
6pm–9pm; Sunday 12pm–3.30pm,
7pm–9pm

14. HOLLINGBOURNE, THE NORTH DOWNS WAY & THURNHAM

All Saints' Church
Upper Street, Hollingbourne, Maidstone,
Kent, ME17 1UN
Tel: 01622 880243
www.achurchnearyou.com/
hollingbourne-all-saints
Opening hours: see website

The Black Horse Inn PH
Pilgrims' Way, Thurnham, Kent, ME14 3LD
Tel: 01622 737185
www.wellieboot.net/home_blackhorse.htm
Food-serving times: Monday–Saturday
12pm–10pm; Sunday 12pm–9pm

Church of St Mary the Virgin
Thurnham, Maidstone, Kent
Tel: see website
www.achurchnearyou.com/thurnham-st-
mary-the-virgin/

Dirty Habit PH
Pilgrims' Way/Upper Street, Hollingbourne,
Maidstone, Kent, ME17 1UW
Tel: 01622 880880
www.elitepubs.com/the_dirtyhabit
Food-serving times: Monday–Friday
12pm–3pm, 6pm–9.45pm; Saturday
12pm–9.45pm; Sunday 12pm–9.30pm

North Downs Way National Trail
Tel: 01622 221525 (North Downs Way
project manager)
www.nationaltrail.co.uk/northdowns

15. NEWINGTON, LOWER HALSTOW & THE MEDWAY ESTUARY

Church of St Mary the Virgin
Newington
Tel: 01795 844241 (keyholder – Rev. Liz Cox; email: rev.liz.cox@btinternet.com)
www.thesix.org.uk

Crown Inn
9 The Street, Upchurch, Sittingbourne, Kent, ME9 7EU
Tel: 01634 233896
Food-serving times: daily 12pm–2pm

St Margaret of Antioch
Lower Halstow
Tel: 01795 842557 (keyholder – Rev. Jacky Davies; email: jackytd@halstowmillhouse.eclipse.co.uk)
www.thesix.org.uk

St Mary's Church
Upchurch
Contact details for key see St Margaret of Antioch, Lower Halstow above
www.thesix.org.uk

Three Tuns
The Street, Lower Halstow, Sittingbourne, Kent, ME9 7DY
Tel: 01795 842840
www.thethreetunsrestaurant.co.uk
Food-serving times: Monday–Saturday 12pm–2pm, 6pm–9pm; Sunday 12pm–9pm

16. BOROUGH GREEN, IGHTHAM MOTE & OLDBURY HILL FORT

George and Dragon
The Street, Ightham, Kent, TN15 9HH
Tel: 01732 882440
www.shepherdneame.co.uk/pub/ightham/george-and-dragon.aspx
Opening hours: daily 11am–11pm

Ightham Mote
Mote Road, Ivy Hatch, Sevenoaks, Kent, TN15 0NT
Tel: 01732 810378, ext. 100 (National Trust)
www.nationaltrust.org.uk
Opening hours: see website

Mote Restaurant
Ightham Mote (see above for full address)
Tel: 01732 811314
Opening hours: call on above number for details of opening times, booking, functions and Christmas lunch

17. HEVER & CHIDDINGSTONE

Castle Inn
Chiddingstone, Edenbridge, Kent, TN8 7AH
Tel: 01892 870247
www.castleinn-kent.co.uk
Food-serving times: Monday–Saturday 12pm–2pm (Saturday 4pm), 7pm–9.30pm; Sunday 12pm–4pm

Chiddingstone Castle
Nr Edenbridge, Kent, TN8 7AD
Tel: 01892 870347
www.chiddingstonecastle.org.uk
Opening hours: see website

Hever Castle
The Estate Office, Hever Castle, Hever, nr Edenbridge, Kent, TN8 7NG
Tel: 01732 865224
www.hevercastle.co.uk
Opening hours: see website

King Henry VIII Inn
Hever Road, Hever, Edenbridge, Kent, TN8 7NH
Tel: 01732 862457
www.kinghenryviiiinn.co.uk
Food-serving times: no food served Monday; Tuesday–Saturday 12pm–3.45pm, 6.30pm–9pm; Sunday 12pm–6pm

Rock Inn
Chiddingstone Heath,
Edenbridge, Kent
Tel: 01892 870296
Food-serving times: Monday 12pm–3.30pm
(drinks/sandwiches only); Tuesday–
Saturday 12pm–2.30pm and 6.30pm–9pm;
Sunday 12pm–4pm

St Mary's Church
High Street, Chiddingstone, Edenbridge,
Kent, TN8 7AH
Tel: 01892 870478
www.achurchnearyou.com/chiddingstone-
st-mary

St Peter's Church
Hever Road, Hever, Kent, TN8 7NH
Tel: see website
www.3spires.org.uk/StPeters.html
Opening hours: daily, usually from
10am–3pm during winter months and
10am–dusk during summer months

18. DORMANSLAND, HAXTED MILL & LINGFIELD

Church of St Peter and St Paul
Church Road, Lingfield,
Gatwick, Surrey
Tel: see website
www.lingfieldparishchurch.org/
Opening hours: daily during daylight hours

Haxted Watermill and Haxted Mill Riverside Brasserie
Haxted Road, Edenbridge,
Kent, TN8 6PU
Tel: 01732 862914
www.haxtedmill.co.uk
Opening hours:
Watermill Easter–September:
Tuesday–Sunday 10am–2.45pm;
October–Easter: Sunday 10am–2.45pm.
Brasserie May–September: Tuesday–Sunday
lunch & dinner; October–April:
Wednesday–Sunday lunch and dinner

Plough Inn
44 Plough Road, Dormansland,
Surrey, RH7 6PS
Tel: 01342 832933
www.ploughdormansland.com
Food-serving times: Monday–Saturday
lunch and dinner; Sunday lunch only. (Thai
meals served Monday–Saturday, English
lunches served Tuesday–Sunday)

Star Inn
Church Road, Lingfield, Surrey, RH7 6AH
Tel: 01342 832364
www.thestar-lingfield.co.uk
Opening hours: Monday–Saturday from
11am; Sunday from 12pm

19. BALCOMBE, ARDINGLY RESERVOIR & WAKEHURST PLACE

Ardingly Reservoir
The Lodge, Ardingly, West Sussex
Tel: 01444 892549
www.ardinglyactivitycentre.co.uk

Balcombe Tea Rooms
Bramble Hill, Balcombe,
Sussex, RH17 6HR
Tel: 01444 811777
www.thebalcombetearooms.co.uk
Opening hours: Tuesday–Saturday
10am–4pm; Sunday 10.30am–4pm

Half Moon PH
Haywards Heath Road, Balcombe,
West Sussex, RH17 6PA
Tel: 01444 811582
www.halfmoonbalcombe.co.uk
Food-serving times: daily 12pm–2.30pm,
7pm–9.30pm

St Peter's Church
Street Lane, Ardingly,
Haywards Heath, West Sussex, RH17 6UR
www.ardinglychurch.co.uk
Opening hours: by arrangement with
rectory; details posted at church

Wakehurst Place Royal Botanic Gardens and Mansion
Ardingly, Nr Haywards Heath,
West Sussex, RH17 6TN
Tel: 01444 894066
www.kew.org/visit-wakehurst
Opening hours: see website

20. POLESDEN LACEY & RANMORE COMMON

Polesden Lacey
Great Bookham, Nr Dorking,
Surrey, RH5 6BD
Tel: 01372 452048
www.nationaltrust.org.uk
Opening hours: see website

Ranmore Common
Nr Dorking, Surrey
Tel: 0844 800 1895 (National Trust)
www.nationaltrust.org.uk

Stepping Stones PH
Westhumble Street, Westhumble,
Nr Dorking, Surrey, RH5 6BS
Tel: 01306 889932
www.steppingstonesdorking.com
Food-serving times: daily 12pm–2.30pm;
Monday–Thursday 7pm–9pm; Friday and
Saturday 7pm–9.30pm

Westhumble Chapel ruin
Westhumble, Nr Dorking, Surrey
Tel: 01372 453401 (National Trust)
www.nationaltrust.org.uk

21. SHERE, THE NORTH DOWNS WAY, ST MARTHA-ON-THE-HILL & THE PILGRIMS' WAY

Church of St Martha-on-the-Hill
Tillingbourne Valley, Guildford, Surrey
www.christchurchguildford.com/index.php?
page=st-martha-s
Opening hours: see website

New Barn Coffee Shop
Newlands Corner, Shere Road, Guildford,
Surrey, GU4 8SE
Tel: 01483 222820
www.thebarnnewlandscorner.co.uk
Opening hours: daily 9am–5pm

Newlands Corner Countryside Centre
Guildford Road, Nr Albury,
Guildford, Surrey
Tel: 01483 517595
Opening hours: daily, staffed on Sunday

North Downs Way National Trail
Tel: 01622 221525 (North Downs Way
project manager)
www.nationaltrail.co.uk

St James's Church
Shere, Guildford, Surrey
Tel: see website
www.achurchnearyou.com/shere-st-james/
Opening hours: daily 8am–dusk

White Horse PH
Middle Street, Shere, Guildford, Surrey
Tel: 01483 202518
www.chefandbrewer.com/pub-food/white-
horse-shere/pid-C0347
Food-serving times: all day

22. BETCHWORTH, BROCKHAM, BUCKLAND & THE RIVER MOLE

The Dolphin
The Street, Betchworth, Surrey, RH3 7DW
Tel: 01737 842288
www.dolphinbetchworth.com
Food-serving hours: Monday–Saturday
12pm–9.30pm; Sunday 12pm–8pm

The Red Lion
Old Reigate Road, Betchworth,
Surrey, RH3 7DS
Tel: 01737 843336
www.redlionbetchworth.co.uk
Food-serving times: Monday–Thursday

12pm–2.30pm, 6.30pm–9pm; Friday
12pm–2.30pm, 6.30pm–9.30pm; Saturday
1pm–4pm, 6.30pm–9.30pm; Sunday
12pm–4pm, 6pm–8pm

23. LISS, SELBORNE & THE HANGERS WAY

Gilbert White's House and Garden and The Oates Museum
High Street, Selborne,
Hampshire, GU34 3JH
Tel: 01420 511275
www.gilbertwhiteshouse.org.uk
Opening hours: see website

Hawkley Inn
Pocock's Lane, Hawkley,
Liss, Hampshire, GU33 6NE
Tel: 01730 827205
www.hawkleyinn.co.uk
Food-serving hours: daily for lunch and
dinner, except Sunday evenings

Queens at Selborne
Queens Hotel, High Street, Selborne,
Hampshire, GU34 3JJ
Tel: 01420 511454
www.thequeensatselborne.co.uk
Food-serving times: Tuesday–Saturday
12pm–3pm, 7pm–10.30pm; Sunday
12pm–5pm

Selborne Arms
High Street, Selborne,
Hampshire, GU34 3JR
Tel: 01420 511247
www.selbornearms.co.uk
Food-serving times: daily 12pm–2pm,
7pm–9pm (Sunday 8.30pm)

24. OVERTON, HANNINGTON & WATERSHIP DOWN

The Vine at Hannington
Hannington, Tadley, Hampshire, RG26 5TX
Tel: 01635 298525
www.thevineathannington.co.uk
Food-serving times: Monday–Friday
12pm–2pm, 6pm–9pm; Saturday
12pm–2.30pm, 6pm–9pm; Sunday
12pm–8pm

25. STRATFIELD MORTIMER, SILCHESTER ROMAN TOWN & THE DEVIL'S HIGHWAY

Cinnamon Tree
The Street, Stratfield Mortimer,
Berkshire, RG7 3NR
Tel: 0118 933 2428
www.cinnamontreemortimer.co.uk
Food-serving times: Monday–Saturday
12pm–2.30pm, 6pm–11pm; Sunday
1pm–5pm, 6pm–11pm

St Mary's Church
The Street, Stratfield Mortimer, Berkshire
Tel: 0118 933 3704 (church wardens)
Opening hours: by arrangement with
church wardens

INDEX

Index

Index

ACKNOWLEDGEMENTS

The author, Christopher Somerville, would like to thank Ruth, who braved the rude wind's wild lament (and the bitter weather) to check these walks.

Picture Credits
All photographs by the author with the exception of the following:
Front Cover: North Downs Way looking toward the South Downs in Sussex, © incamerastock / Alamy.
Back Cover: Autumnal Woodland at Berkhamsted Common, © Helen Dixon / Alamy.
Pp. 9, 85, 93 (top), 93 (bottom), 99, 107 (top), 107 (bottom), 159 and 191 (bottom): © Shutterstock.
P. 13: © Greg Balfour Evans / Alamy.
Pp. 21 and 143: © istockphoto.com.
P. 51: © Bhandol / Alamy.
P. 55: © Chris Howe / Alamy.
P. 63: © Angelo Hornak / Alamy.
P. 69: © ImageState / Alamy.
P.77: © Timothy Smith / Alamy.
Pp.151 and 167 (bottom): © Robert Harding Picture Library Ltd / Alamy.
P. 179: © Simon Tranter Photography / Alamy.